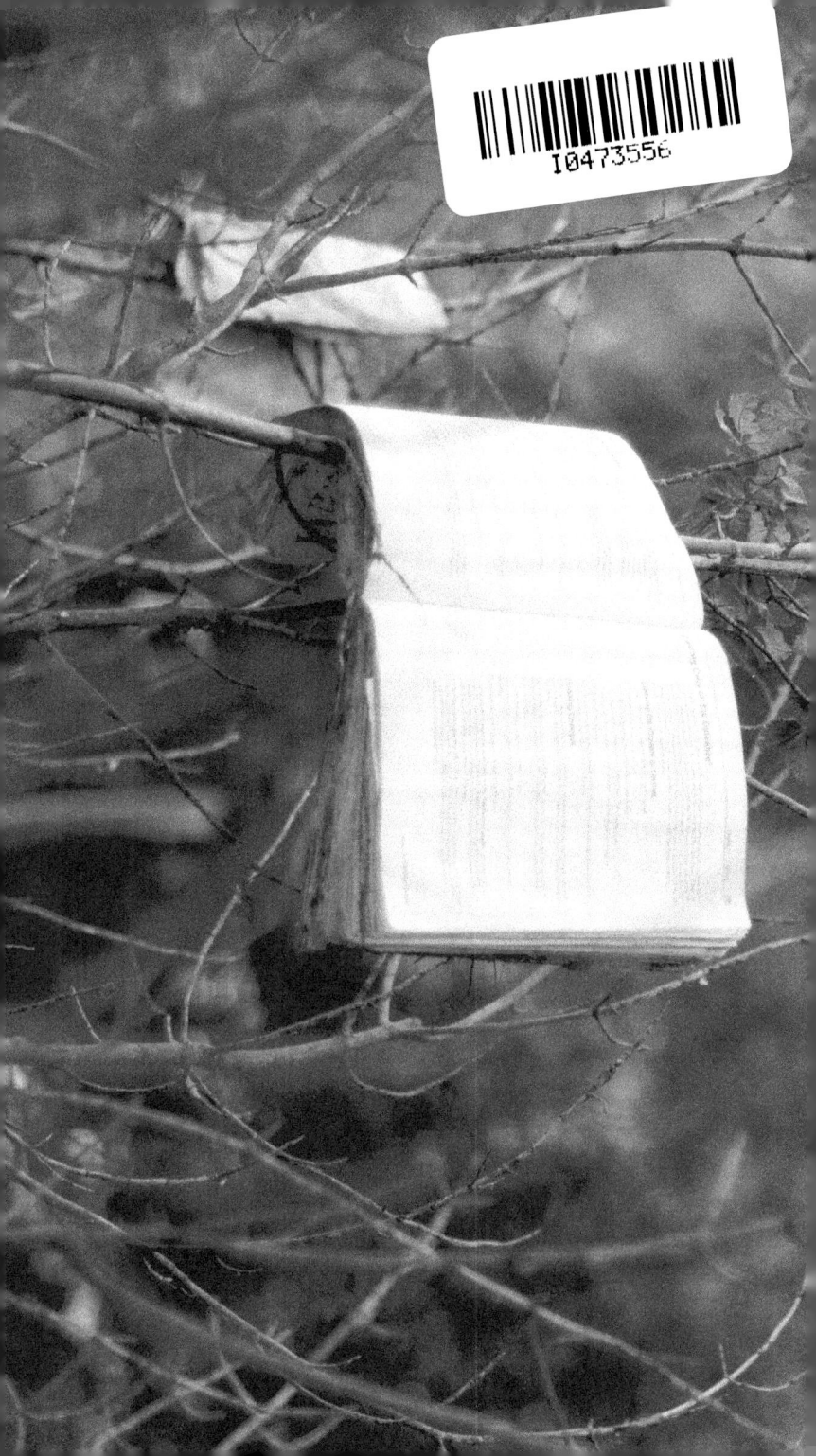

Codex

Micah Bloom

The Digital Press at the University of North Dakota

How to Use This Book

This book is part of the larger *Codex* project initiated by Micah Bloom in the aftermath of the 2011 Minot, ND flood. It is possible to enjoy this book on its own merits, but we also encourage you to read online, or download, the complete, color version of *Codex*, available by the link at the bottom of this page. We would also urge you to view the award-winning film, *Codex*, which documents the fate of the books swept away by the Souris River. The transmedia experience of *Codex* is recommended for a deeper understanding of the project's meditation on the book.

View the *Codex* film:

Codex Film, 40 minutes:
https://archive.org/details/BloomCODEX40

Codex Film, 20 minutes:
https://archive.org/details/BloomCODEX20

View the complete *Codex* book in color:

https://archive.org/details/BloomCodex

Dedicated to those who faced the great of flood 2011

Many waters cannot quench love, neither can the floods drown it.
Song of Solomon 8:7

Photographs by Micah Bloom and Codex team

Design and Layout : Micah Bloom and Marissa Dyke

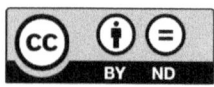

The Digital Press at the University of North Dakota 2017

Acknowledgements
Special thanks to my wife, Sara, and our children: Eva, Magdalana, Aletheia, Valorosa and Zacchaeus. They sacrificed the most for this work, and also provided the most encouragement.

I am grateful for the assistance of my fellow colleagues, and students, at Minot State University, Minot, North Dakota. Without them these are all but blank pages.

These essays were copy-edited by the students in David Haeselin's writing, editing, and publishing course at the University of North Dakota and by Susan Caraher. This book is published by The Digital Press at the University of North Dakota (UND), under the direction of Bill Caraher, with funding from UND, North Dakota Humanities Council and Minot State University.

Library of Congress Control Number: 2017917122
Digital Press at The University of North Dakota, The, Grand Forks, ND

ISBN-13: 978-0692978269 (Digital Press at The University of North Dakota, The)
ISBN-10: 0692978267

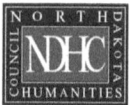

Contents

Archaeologists study formation processes. These are the various natural and cultural processes that transform human activity into archaeological sites. To make meaning from the physical traces of the past, archaeologists disentangle the various events that create what we see in the present. The result of this work is both an appreciation for the complexity of time and an understanding of objects, that within specific contexts, co-produce meaning.

The surging waters of the 2011 Souris River flood left the city of Minot, North Dakota coated in mud and strewn with debris. Beyond the typical documentation of the flood's effects, Micah Bloom's camera, focused particularly on the books that the river deposited across the landscape. Bloom's *Codex*, presents that moment and its aftermath through arresting photographs and a film of those books that endured the inundation. This volume captures formation processes and expands upon *Codex* with a series of new essays.

I became familiar with Bloom's project during its installation at the North Dakota Museum of Art in May of 2015. **Laurel Reuter**'s essay provides a perspective on that event from her position as director of the museum. The exhibit combined his photographs with various approaches to dealing with the damaged and waterlogged books. Some approaches were archaeological and featured careful indexing, systematic photography, and precise scientific documentation. Others approaches embraced a religious cast, manifest in a neatly-arranged book cemetery commemorating each volume lost.

Setting the stage, **Bethany Andreasen**'s contribution provides a sweeping overview of the natural events that precipitated the historic, water crisis. **Robert Kibler** posits the work of the flood and Bloom's work has produced a tenable intersection that requires both natural and human transformations. As **Ryan Stander** uncovers, historic photographs of war echo both the book-littered landscape of the post-flood Souris and the artists desire to remind humanity of the sobering realities of mortality.

In many ways, formation processes also produce books. **Thora Brylowe** reminds us that books themselves emerge from natural processes mediated by human intentions. **Sheila Liming**'s essay reveals that books are always in the process of decomposition as both the physical objects and the ephemeral containers of ideas. Bloom's lens presents blurred words and water-soaked pages and encourages us to recognize that the intent of the book is, as **Justin Sorensen** writes, part of what gives it meaning. Books are to be read, but even when they're not readable, they still speak to us as artifacts. The meaning of the books in Bloom's *Codex* compels us to take their materiality seriously and to recognize, using **David Haeselin**'s term, that they are *constructed*. As **Brian Prugh**'s essay notes, books are "a more human kind of thing"- they are special objects.

This book too was constructed in a particular way. The contributors hail from around the U.S. and bring a range of perspectives from the fields of history, literature, art history, and criticism to Bloom's work. Their responses to Bloom's *Codex* situates his work within the humanities and by doing so creates new and diverse meaning for his multi-media artwork. This book reminds us that formation processes do more than make archaeological sites, but also offer rich contexts for understanding our past and our present. Offering new contexts for viewing both Micah Bloom's work and the 2011 Minot flood, this volume encourages others to form new meaning from these images, essays, and events.

– William Caraher

The Digital Press at the University of North Dakota

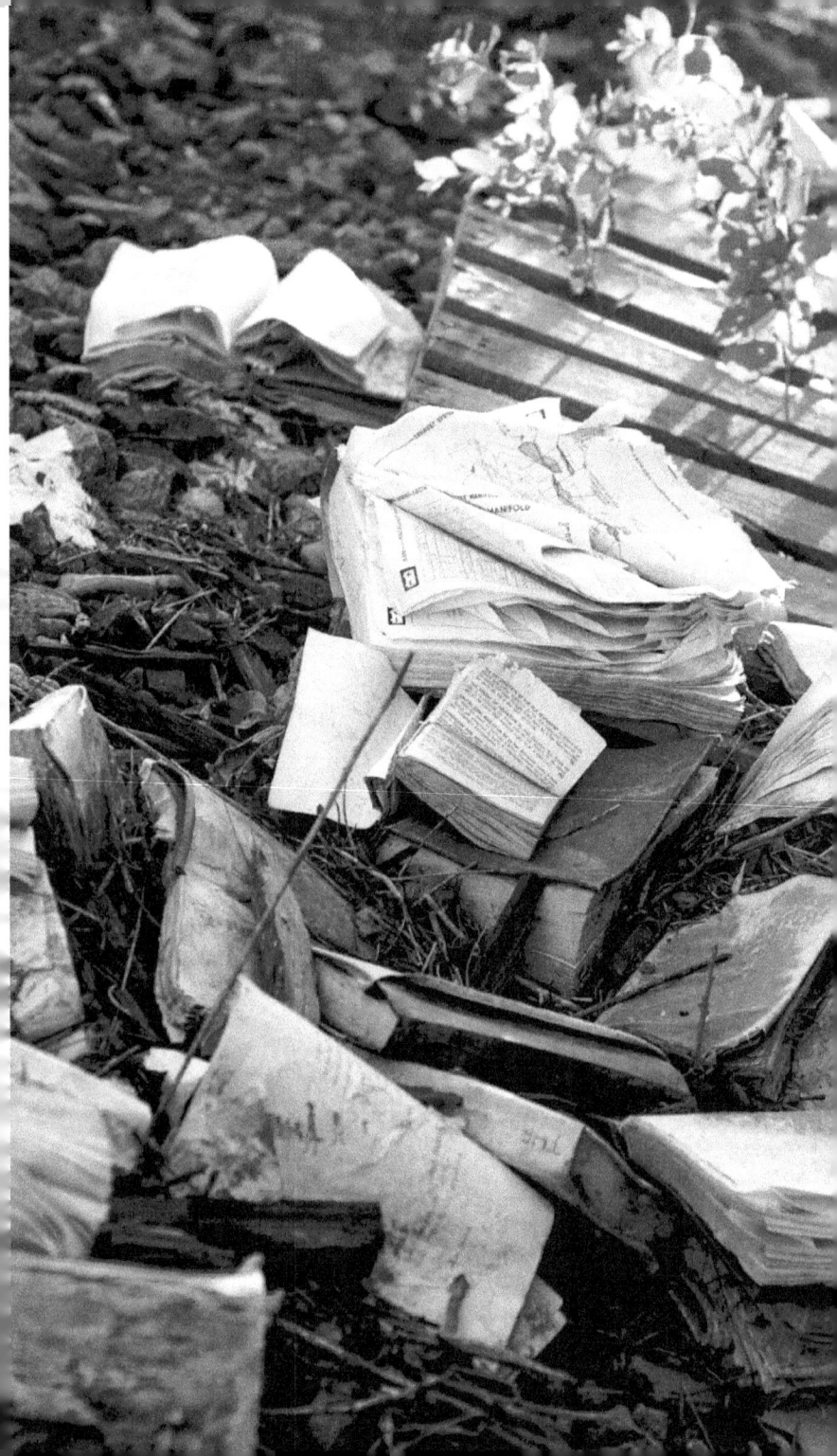

ALL THE STORIES WE KNOW

all the stories we know
eventually become earth
the whispered secret
the tender ribbon of love
the march of armies
the recipe for bread

although sometimes
they echo like the
concentric circles of
a pebble dropped
in watery memory

or combust
turning grief
into heat
then light
then air

only to rain on us again
the everyday alphabet of
trying to understand this life
each wet letter
bequeathing us
promise and admonition
lock and key
flesh and thread
and light enough to work

– ShaunAnne Tangney

Codex

Micah Bloom: Codex
Laurel Reuter

Laurel Reuter: I was the only one I knew who took my library to college with me. One cardboard box of treasured books.

Micah Bloom: When I was a child, my parents instilled in me a reverence for books. They were not to be stepped on, sat upon or abused, because they contained something mysterious and powerful.

Laurel Reuter: December 24, 2015, my gift didn't arrive for seven-year-old Zane. What to do? I rummaged through the children's shelves in my grown-up library and settled upon Ogden Nash's *Zoo*. Ecstatic, Zane clutched it to his chest all afternoon. "This is my favorite Christmas present!"

Micah Bloom: In our home, books were elevated in the hierarchy of objects; in their nature, deemed closer to humans than furniture, knickknacks, or clothing.

Laurel Reuter: August 2016, Zane spent a week with me while attending Art Camp, gradually coming to know the house. He mused while lounging in the window seat in my library, "Why am I most comfortable in this room?"

Micah Bloom: Beyond their mere physical composition of wood fibers and ink, they played some indispensable role that demanded respect and preservation. In a magical way, they were carriers of that which was irreplaceable; they housed an intellect, a unique soul.

Laurel Reuter: Winter 1997, storm after storm dumped snow on the already saturated ground. On April 4, the most brutal blizzard of all started with rain that turned to sleet and culminated in twenty inches of wet snow. Grand Forks, North Dakota, at the convergence of two great muddy rivers, the Red and the Red Lake River, was set for a flood of unremembered proportions.

Micah Bloom: June 22, 2011, the Souris River ravaged Minot, North Dakota. Forcing its way through homes, it seized thousands of precious items carrying them to new resting places. Foremost among the displaced were hundreds, possibly thousands, of books. These books were pilfered from shelves, floated through broken windows, and recklessly abandoned to fend off the natural elements.

MICAH BLOOM: *CODEX*

Minot, like Grand Forks, is a university town. Books, the bedrock of intellectual life, are tucked into private libraries and studies, basements, bedsides, and every which where. Essential tools of learning were disgorged by the rising water of the Souris—as happened with the Red and the Red Lake rivers—into mountains of trash lining berms and streets, and overwhelming landfills.

In Micah Bloom's *Codex*, his reverence for the object is palpable, it nudges the viewer to remember a long and precious human love affair with books. Photographs of tattered book pages aloft in trees speak of more than an image of a plastic bag or a piece of paper tossed by the wind into the branches of a tree. One is taken aback. It is a book. Its words and meanings disappeared; its spirit lingers.

The artist collected such damaged books and re-pulped them into the slurry that becomes new sheets of paper, wherein he embedded his photographic images of destroyed books. These became the new works of art that line three walls of his exhibition *Codex* and fill the pages of his new book *Codex*.

In the exhibition, the floor or ground is piled with dirt, a mixture of sand and loam intended to emulate Minot's soil. Books wrapped in white paper are placed in a grid atop the soil. The dirt, which sometimes spills onto the packaged books, is visually foiled by an abandoned shovel.

Echoing on the fourth wall is an additional grid formed by hundreds of pinned-up Polaroid photos of damaged books taken as Micah Bloom came upon them in the aftermath of the flood. Books, books, books are everywhere in this formally composed exhibition of books in shambles, in disorder and destruction. The endless recycling, contraction, and expansion of human life is at the core of Bloom's art. The fragility of knowledge is underscored by the packaged books returning to earth, by whole libraries consumed by water.

In the Grand Forks 1997 flood, Eliot's Twice Told Tales store flooded and then burned. In Minot, some books, and the idea of books, were rescued through Micah Bloom's art.

CBS News Sunday trailed me as I returned after the flood. We were standing on the site of Eliot Glassheim's vanished bookstore. The interviewer bent over, picked up the closest book, flipped it over to find its title: *Twenty Thousand Leagues Under the Sea.*

The artwork, however, is not just about a flood and the derailment of intellectual life. The artist draws upon visual language to capture the essence of books as they evolved alongside civilization. For some 4,500 years, handmade clay tablets, scrolls and sheets of papyrus, vellum, and bark bore the records of whole peoples, their accounts and lists, histories and philosophies, as well as their deepest longings. They were to be replaced millenniums later by hand bound, expensive, and elaborate books, called codices, only available to the tiniest elite. It wasn't until around 100 AD that the Chinese took hemp rags and mulberry bark and invented paper.

It took another fifteen-hundred years for papermaking to circumnavigate the world. Again, it was the Chinese, with their 3,000-year history of wood carving, who invented movable type carved from wood (around 650 AD). It wasn't, however, until a thousand years later the Johannes Gutenberg created movable metal type to print the first codices—or books—in large numbers. Beautiful, precious, illustrated scrolls had been copied by scribes; the Gutenberg Bible heralded the mass production of books.

Bloom's photographs of damaged books, whose structures have erupted into cascading pages and tumbling forms, suggest mysteries from this hidden past that seem to lay within the subconscious. But isn't that what art is supposed to do?

Some might speculate that my now eight-year-old Zane's intuitive understanding of the bond between books and human life arose from his collective unconscious. The Library of Alexandria, constructed in the third century BC, housed one of the most significant collections of papyrus scrolls in the ancient world. Its destruction has become a universal symbol for the loss of cultural knowledge. Micah Bloom's determination to excavate the damaged books in remote Minot, North Dakota, and to give them life anew harks back to ancient history reinforced by the teachings of his childhood. Humans will not let go of their own history. E-books are carriers of words. Works of art, like books, can embody everything.

Facing Floods: Minot and The Mouse River
Bethany Andreasen

Minot, North Dakota came into existence when the Great Northern Railroad opened a depot in a valley on the south side of the Mouse River (also known, mainly in Canada, as the Souris River) in northwest North Dakota in October of 1886. Normally a relatively small and slow-moving stream, the Mouse originates in Saskatchewan, flows through a large oxbow in North Dakota, then returns to Canada in Manitoba, where it empties into the Assiniboine. Incorporated in July of 1887, the city of Minot grew quickly, eventually expanding through the valley and into the surrounding hills, incorporating the settlement of Harrison on the north side of the river.

As a creation of the railroad, Minot never relied upon the Mouse for transportation, beyond the water and lumber that the river and its banks provided for construction and operation of the railroads. In fact, the river served as an obstacle to transportation; years passed before the city had constructed many bridges across the river. What the river did contribute to the city was ice harvesting (until the 1950s) and recreation. Boating excursions on the river served as popular outings, and connected the city's residents with its riverside parks. Swimming and fishing brought people to the river in the summer, while opportunities for ice skating and hockey beckoned in the winter.

Every so often, however, fed by winter snows, spring melts, and heavy rains, the river changed its nature and overflowed its banks. Through the first two-thirds of the twentieth century, every generation of Minot experienced major flooding, sometimes during several years in quick succession. The flood of 1904, which reached water levels unequaled during the remainder of the twentieth century, took hold overnight, and forced residents to scurry to find or build boats and rafts to rescue stranded citizens from their homes. The year 1916 brought the next flood, while the decade of the 1920s saw three, along with an effort to build up the city's dikes. The worst of these, in 1923, destroyed the local ice company, unleashing 7000 tons of ice that wreaked havoc for miles downstream until they finally melted.

In the arid 1930s, flooding was not an immediate concern, but during that decade, the federal government purchased land upstream which became the Upper Souris Wildlife Refuge, and ultimately included the creation of Lake Darling, with dikes and water control structures intended to establish control over the river's flow. While Minot's population nearly doubled between 1940 and 1970, a sense of complacency about the possibility of flooding developed on the part of the city's citizens. The three floods that did affect the city between 1948 and 1951 were lesser events that did not pose significant challenges. With concern about flooding declining and in response to the population increase during the 1950s and 1960s, optimistic residents constructed ever more structures in areas at least theoretically vulnerable to high waters.

Then came the flood of 1969. Winter snow accumulations significantly above average (totaling over fifty inches in Minot), some arriving in late winter, began to melt rapidly due to high temperatures in early April. The Des Lacs River, which flows into the Mouse a few miles northwest of Minot, threatened to push that river beyond its banks in Minot in early April. Private diking began in Minot on Easter Sunday, April 6; the river began to flood the city the next day. Amid hurried diking and sandbagging, hundreds of citizens packed up and moved prized possessions as they evacuated their homes.

The river crested on April 11, but just as it began to

recede, the United States Army Corps of Engineers warned that an even larger flood crest was heading downstream from the overflowing reservoir at Lake Darling. A second, larger evacuation began; more than 11,000 people, constituting a third of the city's population, relocated from their homes. Broadway, the main north-south artery, was built up by as much as nine feet in order to preserve a route across the river, but only vehicles with special permits could use it, while others drove a fifteen mile route through the country to reach the other side of the city. Much of the city remained under water for weeks. Recovery efforts finally began when the river returned to its banks on May 15.

Spring flooding and evacuation became an almost annual event in the 1970s, but the city mostly succeeded in maintaining control of the crests. During that decade, the Corps of Engineers undertook the Minot Channel Improvement Project, which included efforts to speed the river's travel through Minot by clearing the river of fallen trees and other obstacles, as well as constructing cutoffs intended to straighten its channel. The Corps built permanent dikes along the river's path through the city. Also, between 1988 and 1995, construction of the Rafferty and Alameda Dams on the Souris in Saskatchewan (funded in large part by American dollars) furthered these flood protection efforts, as did an improved dam and water control structure at Lake Darling. By the end of the twentieth century, most Minot residents assumed that these efforts had permanently removed the threat of a serious flood. Financial institutions no longer required flood insurance for most homes or businesses located in the flood plain.

For years, those assumptions seemed justified. But in 2010 and 2011, conditions came together that transformed the unthinkable into reality. Substantial precipitation saturated the soil in the drainage area of the Mouse during the fall of 2010, and water levels in lakes and sloughs were high. The winter of 2010-2011 brought heavy snow. Running at unusually high water levels, the reservoirs began releasing water downstream in early January, but as the melt began in the spring, the reservoirs refilled quickly. The National Weather Service announced that these conditions made high spring river levels extremely likely. Then, heavy rains in late May forced the reservoirs to release larger flows. On May 20, the city began to build barriers along 4th Avenue NW, and on May 24, it secured the services of the Corps of Engineers, which began working on dike improvements the next day.

The first crisis came, as it had in 1969, due to rising levels on the Des Lacs; on May 31, the Corps predicted flooding in Minot. The next day, the city ordered mandatory evacuation of structures close to the river; residents rushed to sandbag their homes, bring up items from their basements, and pack some of their possessions to move them beyond danger. The Des Lacs rose seven feet over a period of 24 hours, but the diking held, and wet basements remained the city's major problem. A few days later, evacuees were allowed to return, and some of the newly constructed dikes were removed. Minot breathed a sigh of relief.

But the releases from the upriver dams on the Mouse were still high, as their managers attempted to balance the problems this would create for downstream locations with the need to prepare their reservoirs to handle the possibility of additional precipitation. The National Weather Service warned that heavy rainfall could cause another rise in the river; such a rainfall occurred throughout the river's drainage area in mid-June. It was no longer possible to deny that a flood was imminent, and Minot returned to sandbagging and dike building to prepare for the new emergency. The only question was how high the water would be. Minot residents who remembered the flood of 1969, as well as those who only knew it secondhand through the lore that had grown in its wake, assumed that nothing could be worse than that flood had been. Official predictions that the water level would be seven to eight feet higher than in 1969 seemed unbelievable.

On June 20, the city ordered evacuation for those in the flood plain, to be completed by 10:00 p.m. on June 22. Shelters opened at several locations to house the newly homeless. Residents resumed the process of moving, packing, and sandbagging, gratefully accepting the assistance of others who volunteered their help and their vehicles. The evacuation deadline was moved up to 6:00 p.m., but the siren signaling that the river had begun to overflow the levees sounded at 12:57 p.m. The water rose the next several days until it crested on June 25.

It took weeks for the water to recede. During that time, the people of Minot adjusted to a new normal. More than 4000 homes were evacuated, but in the end, only about 350 people stayed in the shelters, as most of the rest were taken in by friends or relatives, or camped near the ice arena. Residents spent hours watching non-stop coverage of the flood by the local television stations, with aerial film offering the only way to view the full scope of the disaster. The Blackhawk helicopters of the National Guard continually passed overhead. When the city's sewage treatment plant was compromised, citizens followed the order to boil water for personal consumption. Those who lived on the north side of town had to travel to the other side of the river to access medical care facilities and grocery stores, until limited versions of such services were established in northern locations. A trip to the other side of town, normally a matter of minutes, could now take more than an hour due to heavy traffic on the single north-south route open to the public.

Gradually, as the weeks passed, the water receded, and the work of recovery began. Returning to their homes, evacuees found a thick layer of mud covering their floors and lawns, and debris everywhere. Heavy water flow had moved everything that wasn't nailed down, and much that was. The flood pushed some houses off their foundations, and many smaller buildings and decks traveled downstream until they came to rest against a larger obstacle. Smaller personal possessions washed out of homes through broken windows and lay scattered along the flooding river's path.

Today in 2017, more than five years after the flood, visible evidence of the disaster remains, especially in the form of so-called "zombie houses," left behind by owners who have not undertaken the challenge of restoring them. But the invisible impact is even greater, in that no one in Minot remains complacent about the threat of flooding. An effort to construct more massive flood prevention structures has barely begun to move beyond the planning stages. Heavy snowfall during the early part of the winter of 2016-2017 raised the flood risk for the river basin far above normal, and the people of Minot watched and waited with concern until it was clear that the decline of snowfall in the latter part of the winter had removed the threat.

The books that Micah Bloom has discovered and photographed bear their own witness to the disaster and its aftermath. They stand in for human victims of the flood, set adrift by the water, involuntarily redistributed to new locations, coming out worse for the wear. These books may fall low in priority on the scale of destruction wrought by the flood, but they serve as symbols of the multitude of stories lost to Minot: the doorframe marks denoting the height of the children as they grew, the classroom where a future was first dimly visualized, the church that hosted weddings, baptisms, and funerals for immigrant settlers. And the books' demise, whether brought about through natural decay, burial, or cremation (and what could be more appropriate in a region heavily-populated with Norwegian-Americans than a floating pyre?), serves as metaphor for those for whom the damage of the flood was too severe to do anything other than depart the city and chart a new course.

For Further Reading and Viewing

Anderson, Bruce. *Welcome to Flood City* (DVD). Minot, ND: Sunshine Creations L.L.C., 2012.

Forsberg, Reuben, John Wright, and Frank Phipps. *Mouse That Roared: A Pictorial Review of the Minot Flood*. Minot. ND: Garfunkle Publications, 1969.

Minot-Ward County Centennial Book Committee. "A Brief History of Minot," in Minot-Ward County Centennial Book Committee, *People, Places & Events, Minot, Ward County: Bridging the Century*. Minot, ND: Centennial Book Committee [Minot, ND], 1986.

Minot Daily News. Flood 2011: The Minot Daily News Chronicles the Souris River Flood of 2011. Minot, ND: Pediment Publishing, 2012.

Reiner, Elmer, Ray Kerns, and Gorden Tofte. *Flood "69": Complete Pictorial Coverage Of The 1969 Minot Flood*. Minot, ND: Star Production Co., n.d.

Timbrook, Mark. *The Last Hurrah: An Account of Life in the Mouse River Valley, Bone Town, Little Chicago, and the Magic City*, Minot. ND: Niess Impressions, 2008.

Tompkins, Chuck. *Minot Down Under: A Pictorial of the Great Souris River Flood of 2011*. Minot, ND: Tompkins Publishing, 2011.

The Flood, the Mill, and the Body of the Book
Thora Brylowe

Micah Bloom's photos present to us a beautiful apocalypse. Knowledge has been rendered down to its constituent material form by the sublime forces of nature. The ruined codex stands in for the works, great and small, of all civilized people. Books, little metaphors for the bodies of their authors, lay splayed, abject before the spectator. As our minds are housed in these frail bodies, so our words live between brittle bindings. In these photos, we witness the aftermath of a tragedy as old as culture, for human culture has always required the waters of the river, first to feed our plants and then to turn our machines. But those waters, as the Bloom's photos show, have a way of betraying us. Even now, the destruction of a library somehow evokes a cataclysm as ancient as human knowledge: floods, fire and ice. In time, all recorded history, creativity and science will bloat, shrivel or crack. It will burn or flood or freeze. Human culture is fleeting. Only Earth abides. Despite our careful collecting, curating and research, culture is ultimately subject to the whims of nature. Were it not for the wistful beauty of these dead things, we might be tempted to despair.

The word *culture* comes to us from the same root word as *agriculture*. It was not until the nineteenth century that the word stood for the kind of intellectual corpus stored in books.[1]   Before that, when we thought about culture, we were content to think of the cultivation of crops, not minds. And surely, forces bigger than culture are at work in Bloom's haunting photographs: the mighty river, the air and sea that caused this river to flood its banks. Of course, the water is not present now. Bloom records the brutal aftermath of the rising waters. Here, a book hangs obscenely in a tree. There one lies splayed beneath the lens, a jarring white corpse among the rocks and decaying leaves. We know the river must be somewhere nearby, calm now, made gentle by a seasonal shift in our planet's relationship to its star. Since we humans settled in the Fertile Crescent or along the Yellow River, the waters have alternately sustained and thwarted culture. Rivers fed and hydrated ancient minds and the bodies that contained them. Papyrus was cut from the shallows of the fertile Nile. It was unwrapped and stitched into flat surfaces that recorded some of our earliest civilized art and science.[2]   Yet at the same time, ancient tales of floods abound. They are the stuff of history and of legend. The Hebrew God sent flood waters to wipe clean the excesses of culture. There are flood tales in Australia, China, India, ancient Mesopotamia, and in the Americas. The river gives and the river takes. We recognize the inevitability of this purge.

The Mouse River, also known as the Souris, flows from the Yellow Grass Marshes of Saskatchewan, bending south into North Dakota, and then meandering back north into Manitoba, eventually emptying into the Assiniboine. In June of 2011, the snows that blanketed Saskatchewan melted, overflowing the dams that were meant to contain it and irrigate the surrounding land. Rushing water poured downstream and south into North Dakota, overwhelming the city of Minot and

---

1. Terry Eagleton. *The Idea of Culture.* (Oxford: Blackwell Publishers, 2000), 1.

2. Keith Houston. *The Book: A Cover to Cover Exploration of the Most Powerful Object of our Time.* (New York: W. W. Norton & Company, 2016), 12-3.

forcing the evacuation of its homes. It would be easy to end the tale there, in a flood worse than any on record, in an aftermath of drowned books, forensic scientists inspecting the bodies for evidence of disease or foul play. It would be easy to make Bloom's pictures the story of a river and a town and about their tragedy of dead books. But we are products of our history. Our stories ripple out. The greater world flows in. The flood waters that inundated Minot and cleansed it of its books were a result of a protracted La Niña pattern that developed the year before. La Niña occurs when cool Pacific waters change weather on a global scale. That makes these photographs a story about the sea and the air as much as it is a story about an overflowing river and the books it left tattered and ruined, bleached blank by the emerging summer sun.

Bloom's photographs also tell a story about *culture* in the nineteenth-century use of the term, a culture the great poet and critic Mathew Arnold defined as "sweetness and light."[3] Culture for Arnold consisted of the best that had been thought and written, a "study of perfection" that binds the individual to his social world.[4] Set against the increasingly mechanized and alienating landscape of industrialization, culture offered a respite from mill and machine. For Arnold, it was not England's coal or railroads that made her great. England was great because of its tradition of art, religion, and poetry, works that could inspire a shared sense of moral unity. Of course, these momentous works circulated in books, and the nineteenth century saw the first mechanized production of both paper and print. In 1869, when Arnold published his long essay *Culture and Anarchy*, which objected to "faith in machinery" (both mechanical and social) as a "besetting danger," his culture relied on mechanized printing to reach

3. Matthew Arnold. *Culture and Anarchy and Other Writings.* edited by Stefan Collini. (Cambridge University Press, 1993).

4. Arnold, 59.

the masses; Arnold hoped the rifts in it could be sutured by sweetness and light.[5] Before the invention of wood pulp paper in the 1840s, paper was recycled from rags. But industrialized society, and its new readerly classes, needed a more plentiful and reliable source of material. Around the same time, the rotary steam press revolutionized printing, enabling print runs of up to a thousand impressions an hour. By the 1860s, huge "webs" (or rolls) of paper, like the kind in the books strewn around Minot, unrolled into printing presses, which spat out double-sided sheets at 1200 sheets an hour.[6] As the nineteenth century gave way to the twentieth, paper mills devoured virgin forests, polluted clean water with bleach and stinking chemicals, and pumped carbon dioxide into the sky. Sweetness and light, it would seem, could not survive without its filthy bête noir, the mill.

Rivers run mills. Since culture (in the old sense) began, mills have processed the fruits of the earth into things we can actually use: wheat into flour; corn into meal; cane into sugar. Mills make trees into boards, and, midway through the Industrial Revolution, they also made trees into paper. In Arnold's nineteenth century, the same technology that made steam engines and rotary presses transformed the mill into a massive and efficient machine. Coal-heated steam, not flowing water from the river, turned its works. This transformation brings us to a new place, both in the expansion of culture and in our effects on nature. Scholars of climate change have invented a new word to describe this effect: the *anthropocene* refers to our current geologic epoch. As the prefix "anthro" suggests, scientists believe humans and their activity have affected the workings of the natural world so profoundly that we have wrought permanent changes on the nature of our planet.[7] The

5. Arnold, 65.
6. William Bullock. US Patent # 61996 A. 12 February, 1867.
7. P. J. Crutzen, "Geology of Mankind." Nature 415 (2002): 23.

anthropocene began, many argue, with the invention of the steam engine and the subsequent Industrial Revolution. Coal fires spewed carbon dioxide into the air. Industrial pollutants multiplied. Populations grew. Rivers washed fertilizers into the sea. Trees disappeared at an alarming rate. The planet began to warm.

Although La Niña weather patterns are characterized by cool tropical Pacific waters, 2011 was the warmest La Niña year ever recorded. Climate modeling suggests an uptick in extreme La Niña events due to global warming is highly likely.[8] As I write this in early 2017, we are in the midst of a sustained La Niña pattern that has caused record cold across swathes of the central US and promises above-normal temperatures in Alaska. The National Weather Service's Climate Prediction Center anticipates above normal temperatures across the US and above-median precipitation for the West.[9] Perhaps Matthew Arnold was correct in assessing this besetting danger. Our thirst for machinery has reshaped the Earth's patterns of wind and water. In the anthropocene, the line between nature and culture is difficult to distinguish. If culture cannot exist without its dark counterpart, the industrialized mill, it must affect nature by virtue of the carbon and pollutants that accompany it.

Suddenly Bloom's pictures become a more complex story than a simple encounter between the frailties of refined culture and the apocalyptic contingencies of nature. Paper is

8. Wenju Cai, Guojian Wang, Agus Santoso, Michael J. McPhaden, Lixin Wu, Fei-Fei Jin, Axel Timmermann, Mat Collins, Gabriel Vecchi, Matthieu Lengaigne, Matthew H. England, Dietmar Dommenget, Ken Takahashi & Eric Guilyardi. "Increased frequency of extreme La Niña events under greenhouse warming." *Nature Climate Change* 5 (2015): 132–137.

9. National Weather Service, Climate Prediction Center. "Prognostic Discussion For Long-Lead Seasonal Outlooks." Published 15 December 2016. Available: https://web-beta.archive.org/web/20170501151111 http://www.cpc.ncep.noaa.gov/products/predictions/90day/fxus05.html

the fifth largest global industry, and both nature and culture have paid dearly for our addiction to it. In 2012, each American citizen consumed over five and a half 40-foot trees worth of the stuff.[10] Environmentalists estimate that half of the trees cut in the United States go to paper production.[11] Trees and forests, they point out, are separate things. While *trees* can certainly be replanted, in order to plant a tree "crop," an old-growth forest must first be cut away.[12] In 2005 alone, paper mills put an estimated 500 million tons of carbon into the atmosphere.[13] Anyone who has driven through a town with a papermill knows the distinctive, terrible smell that hovers in the air downwind. The sulfurous, rotten stink comes from the chemical process whereby sulfides and ammonia break down wood into the pulped slurry laid down in thin layers and rolled flat into paper.[14] In the early days of wood pulp paper, wood was mechanically ground, but chemical processes that break down wood into cellulose fibers proved more efficient and yielded more durable paper. With those chemicals came the stink. Wood is not white. In order to make a smooth, white surface, paper must be bleached and sized, processes that involve chlorine bleach and caustic soda, processes that produce as byproducts toxic dioxins and furans. Carbon, pollutants, deforestation. What an irony that paper mills contribute to conditions that caused the Mouse River to flood Minot and ruin its books.

10. Houston, p. 35.

11. Conservatree. "Environmentally Sound Paper Overview: Essential Issues." Available: https://web.archive.orgweb/20170505174328/ http://www. conservatree.org/learn/Essential%20Issues/EIPaperContent.shtml

12. Conservatree.

13. "The paper industry and climate change: Roll on the green revolution: A technological fix is proposed to combat global warming." *The Economist*. 30 November, 2015.

14. Wisconsin Department of Health Services. "Pulp and Paper Industry Odors." 15 December 2015.Available: https://web-beta.archive.org/ web/20170207005827/ https://www.dhs.wisconsin.gov/air/pulpodors.htm

What lessons, then, do Bloom's photographs teach? Culture cannot exist without the mill. Bodies and books, moreover, have long been compared. Books have headnotes, footnotes and (textual) bodies. Portraits of their authors often accompany the text. We are taught to touch books respectfully. We offer them our reverence because they represent—stand in for—the people who wrote them, who might have told us their words themselves, were it not for time and distance and death. We need books to do what bodies cannot: they transcend the inevitable forces of time and distance and death, proffering words we could never otherwise expect to hear. What, then, of these torn and broken bodies scattered through Minot? How do we reconcile culture, a warming planet, an El Niña flood, and the mill with this paper cataclysm? On the surface, a tale of nature versus culture offers comfort because it places "us" on the side of culture and "it"—the terrible, unknowable other—on the side of nature. Nature is the terrible flood, the fire, the tornado or landslide. Culture is the human family that nurtures, cultivates and reads. Nature is the river. Culture is the book. If we delve deeper, however, the flood is really a product of the new human epoch brought on by the mills that warmed the air and changed the sea. Those same mills rendered millions of trees into the paper onto which Minot's books were printed. Manufactured books: the bleached bodies of this new epoch.

The distinction between nature and culture is as murky as the churning waters of the El Niña flood. Regardless of whether we choose to understand this lesson, the waters continue to rise and recede. When the river returns to its banks, we are invariably left with death and ruin. We must consider how to proceed.

(De)Compostition: or, How Matter Matters
Sheila Liming

To modern eyes, books look like garbage about to happen. This is largely because modern people and modern readers have been taught – taught by books, chiefly – to view the component parts of a printed work as dispensable. Paper is cheap to those of us who feed whole reams of it into our printers and copy machines; ink is an afterthought when we can set our Amazon Prime accounts to auto-replenish and receive regular shipments containing neat little cartridges of it; and covers ... well, when was the last time you purchased a *hardback* book, anyway? To the contemporary consumer of the printed word, phrases like "on demand" and "instant download" have reprogramed our brains, compelling us to see the material fact of a book as an immaterial necessity.

But instant gratification is only part of the story. Books also look like garbage about to happen because they are, in fact, a kind of living excrement, formed from castoff or recycled matter and, one feels, destined for still many more go-arounds, with or without us. In this regard, we, the inhabitants of the twenty-first century, are not really unique, for such has been the reputation of print since the rise of cheap paper made from leftover wood ("pulp") in the nineteenth century. Victorians, for instance, excelled in the art of using and reusing and thus also *abusing* paper: they used it to line cupboards and pie plates; they turned it into food wrappers, to cushion cuts of meat or swaddle their fish and chips; they stuffed it into the bottoms of their boots when the leather sprang a leak; and, of course, they took it with them to the privy and put it to work as toilet tissue. Because of its connection to that most unpleasant site of human behavior, Victorians saw print as associated with bodily functions – ingestion, defecation – and not always with the noble works of Shakespeare or Milton. (That, and as anyone who's ever lived near a pulp mill can attest, its method of manufacture also tends to make one think of the privy.)

Micah Bloom's images in *Codex*, I think, bring this long and hallowed history of waste to the fore where print is concerned. In them, print takes on the appearance of decaying vegetation, of decomposing matter, of rotting flesh, even. A certain smell comes wafting off of these images, a smell that everyone knows: dankness, mold, putrefaction. All manner of unholy funk. We can see as well as smell as well as feel the books in the photographs deteriorating, returning to the realm from whence they originally came in a blaze of fungal glory.

The word *decompose* comes from the Latin *decompositus,* and the meaning of that old world antecedent is actually twofold: on the one hand, it refers to the process of separation that occurs when component parts are, via procedural decay, broken apart and disengaged from each other; on the other hand, *decompositus* also refers, somewhat ironically, to the forming of new compounds and bounded wholes. In both the fields of botany and chemistry, for example, the word *decomposite* signifies not degeneration but, rather, addition in identifying a substance or thing that has been, in the words of the *Oxford English Dictionary*, "Further compounded; formed by adding another element or constituent to something already composite."[1]

Books, in a very similar way, invite us to consider the relationship between decomposition as separation and decomposition as compounding. A published book is, after all, a new, compound thing: this fact is registered in the history of the word *novel*, which, in descending from the French *nouvelle*, means, "to make anew." But a book is also a very old thing, a wasted thing, a used up thing. It's comes to us from old trees and leftover scraps and, even, books that once *were* but now, it seems, no longer need *be*.

What's more, we can see that the act of writing a book, of *composing* or *composition*, speaks to this bipartite history of making new and breaking apart. When one sits down to write a book, they do so by combining very old things – scraps of leftover language, phrases they've heard used before, words they think they know. They mold and manipulate and shape those very old things by squeezing them into new arrangements and combinations, some of which seem to fit okay, some of which don't, and some of which come together so seamlessly as to erase the edges of the raw materials that were originally used to create them. These arrangements we call sentences. Or paragraphs. Or chapters. And we stack them up, one upon the other, until we have a brand new book that has the face of a stranger but speaks to us in a voice we can remember from our childhood.

The philosopher Walter Benjamin, in a collection of aphorisms and observations that he published in 1928 called *One-Way Street*, engages with the disposable and seamy side of print's history in comparing it to a prostitute. Books and whores, Benjamin observes, alike come with you to bed; books and whores alike tend to multiply through their own progeny; books and whores can both be found in public establishments, usually sitting next to students; books and whores like to have their fights in public. But perhaps the highlight of this neat little syllogism of Benjamin's is his comment that, with both books and whores, "seldom does one who has possessed them witness their end. They are apt to vanish before they expire."[2] What Bloom's photographs offer us as viewers is a ticket to the show that is that forbidden event: the death, and consequent resurrection, of a book. It feels like a thing that ought to happen quietly, discretely. Yet here it is, happening in the open, with pages splayed and curled, mussed by the indiscriminate hand of a receding tide.

How remarkable. How profane.

Perhaps Benjamin is right, though, and there is something about books that encourages a kind of profane and derisive treatment. Maybe it is all of that history of waste and putrefaction that I have been describing here. Or maybe, on the other hand, it is the way that we are instructed, as schoolchildren, to treat them with respect (even as they seem to whisper to us through the very fact of their materiality and instruct us to do nothing of the sort. Once, I burned my seventh grade math book in my parent's living room fireplace. I can remember the feeling of guilty pleasure that greeted the sight of flames, burning blue and green from the book's plastic cover and full-color diagrams, gobbling it up.)

Like the Souris River, we readers are sometimes guilty of mistreating books: I once left a copy of Edith Wharton's *The Age of Innocence* outside in a rainstorm. I was a on camping trip with some of my graduate school colleagues and I knew that I was doing it, knew that I was placing that book in peril. But it was such a cheap edition, you see, aptly named and issued through the Dover Thrift Edition imprint.[3] I still have that book today for the very fact that the rainstorm ended up making it more personally valuable to me. The rain soaked through the cheap pulp pages and sent my blue ink annotations running left and right over the lines of Wharton's prose. The covers dislodged themselves, in rashness and in desperation, it seemed, and black mold appeared in due time along the edges of the book's spine. But all of this, to my mind, made the skimpy little thing more real and more viable. It had a history now – a history of which I was a part.

I have taken books up mountains, too. I read Jack Kerouac's *Desolation Angels* on top of Desolation Peak in the North Cascades of Washington State, upon the very spot where Kerouac once spent a summer as a paid fire lookout.[4] I tore its front cover off in order to write a note to the man who had delivered me to the foot of that mountain in his motorboat, telling him that he could find me swimming in the cove just around the corner upon his return (and not to leave without me). Now *Desolation Angels* stares at me – coverless and accusatory – from its spot on my bookshelf and silently judges me for these ancient crimes of necessity. In this, it is joined by a copy of Upton Sinclair's *Oil*,[5] which, according to a note that my husband wrote inside of it, sustained rain damage on July 25th, 2009 at Hidden Lake Peak at an elevation of 6900 feet. Like *The Age of Innocence*, it had been left outside, left to fend for itself among the natural elements with which, long before, in forgotten chapters of its previous lives, perhaps, it might have once been on good terms.

Books come to us from nature and nature tries to take them back. In this way, subtle processes of regeneration, recycling, and reclamation mark our interactions with them. When I look at Bloom's photographs, I do not see devastation first and foremost, though it cannot be denied that devastation lurks somewhere on the margins and in the details of each one; rather, I see natural forms slipping free of the arrangements that humans have forced them to assume, if only temporarily.

I see pages returning to dust, mold feasting gluttonously on organic matter, and ink fading on the page and evaporating at last into the atmosphere. In this way, books engender and embody continuous cycles of creation and waste, in the midst of which, we readers are the ones who look temporary, who appear ephemeral.

Bookish
David Haeselin

There's this great little bookshop in Lenox, Massachusetts. The word that comes to mind when I think of it is quintessential. It's located on a tree-lined main street from which you can see the steeples of churches almost as old as the country. Enter the shop, and every square inch of its 500 square feet are covered with books: under the tables, scattered on top of the bookshelves, and piled three-feet high on each side of the register. Jazz plays softly over the stereo. I don't think the vibe is coincidental; this establishment is called "The Bookstore."

Most of the stock is new, but go into the back room past the robust poetry section and the "Get Lit winebar," and you will find a modest selection of used volumes. Back there, as far away as you can get from the entrance, there's one shelf that I find myself drawn to. It's labeled only with a scrap of scotch-taped paper which reads "Thinky Think." These are my kind of books.

As one might expect, the contents of this shelf are motley. Most of the books can be classified as Theory, or more specifically, critical and literary theory. The store's owner probably had difficulty stocking these items because they are all books *about* books. Many of these works question the fundamental logic of Western philosophy, European history, and interpretative traditions in literature, art, music, and popular culture. As a genre, if you can call it that, "thinky think" books are united by taking at least some inspiration from Karl Marx's famous maxim that "Philosophers have hitherto only *interpreted* the world in various ways; the point is to *change* it."[1] These writers all share the conviction that writing about reading could change the world for the better.

---

1. Marx, Karl. "Theses on Feuerbach." *Marxists.org*. 20 May 2017
   https://www.marxists.org/archive/marx/works/1845/theses/

This aspiration has never sounded more naïve. Yet, people on all sides of the political spectrum are profoundly dissatisfied. Many seem to feel that they cannot even imagine ways to make things better. Something is rotten in these United States. It is for that reason that the time is right to reclaim bookishness as a modest yet radical bulwark against the many onslaughts of the "post-factual" world.

Bookishness matters now precisely because reading doesn't. I write this sentence knowing full-well that it smacks of a lament for the good old days. Reading doesn't matter to most people today, but it could. To those who believe in the power of ideas, I suggest that we should not just read more, but we should read more *visibly*.

Micah Bloom's photographs in this collection ask us to look at books. But *Codex* is not just a book about books; it is a book *of* books. More specifically, *Codex* is a Codex full of images of codices, the technical term for a paged-book. The pages of *Codex* remind us that any text or images we place between paper covers can be rightly called a book. And it is the contrast between the mundane and the achingly beautiful that guides my understanding of the work.

By documenting books in the process of destruction, *Codex* shows us that even though books are transcendentally important, they are also food for insects. All books are slowly rotting organic matter. The books featured in *Codex* are just rotting quicker than most. This needn't be a depressing realization. Seeing these images of decay allows me to appreciate how closely linked we humans are to books. When each of us pass, our bodies will be reincorporated into that which nourished us. Our bodies and our books feed the future in ways silicon, glass, and plastic do not. Books are fragile and fleeting, just like their stewards.

The lessons I take from Bloom's photographs are

sometimes unsettling, but I think that is the source of their aesthetic power. Even non-readers could easily produce a list of some of the congratulatory aphorisms about reading that our culture often repeats. Books let us travel through time and space! Books teach us about what it means to be human! Knowledge is power! These clichés can all be true, but the ones Bloom shows us also remind us that books can teach us how to do well on a first date. Books can list rude jokes or insults we can inflict on our friends and enemies. Some books store trivia that is so outdated or fallacious that their obliteration enriches humanity more than their preservation. We mustn't forget that books are various, just like the people who write them and read them.

Bloom's photographs show books that have served too many various purposes to be only romanticized as ideal objects in need of our protection. This doesn't mean that that they aren't worth saving, but to do so, we need to pay attention to these book as specific objects. If we care about the *book qua book* we must fight for it rather than mourn its loss. The technical term librarians use for culling their collections is deaccessioning. To me, Bloom's photographs in Section I show nature's own deaccessioning, exposing how natural processes cut off access to parts of the past. By showing us images of waterlogged, trashed, and all-but-forgotten books, *Codex* asks its reader to stop bluffing about the book's value in the abstract. Instead, it invites us to get down and dirty with books as real things, with paper that was once alive as trees and the leather bindings sometimes as calves or cows. Now these objects live only in the minds of their readers, if at all.

Recently, a friend told me that his wife prohibited him from using paper maps while traveling because it marked him as a tourist, whereas when consulting a map on his phone he "could be doing anything." With a book in your hand, you can only be doing *one thing*. Since the book is designed for one specific, if varied, task, carrying one around makes a statement. Sitting on a park bench with a book means something. Lining your walls with books as the chief decorating strategy for your home or office means something. Cracking one open while bellied up to a bar means something, too; it means that reading matters to you. Now more than ever, we need to make that kind of statement as often as we can. Books shouldn't be prized as relics of a better, smarter time now lost, but as public displays of bookishness that herald a more interesting, civil, and humane future. Whether you are reading *Twilight*, Tolkien, Turgenev or anything in-between, reading in public proclaims a way of being that takes the imagination seriously.

For nearly seventeen-hundred years, the codex has allowed its users to read. Book historians and media theorists are right to remind us that regardless of format, reading has always actually meant a variety of different actions such as skimming, scanning, taking notes in the margins, and orating. Of course, many books contain pictures, charts, and other material that is not read in the same way as text. Reading is not (and has never been) just silent, rapt, "close" or scholarly reading. There are many kinds of books that permit many kinds of reading about all different subjects.

This is the reason I prefer the term bookish over its many synonyms. Learned and erudite, for example, both evoke boring and vague conceptions of the power and practice of reading. Bookish, on the other hand, refers back to the physical object, thereby connecting the object with processes of reading and interpretation. Yet, reading a physical book today means something very different than it did in 1907, 1977, or even 2007, the year Amazon released its Kindle e-reader. In the age of too much of everything, the bookish person is content with way he uses his leisure time to enrich his understanding of the world and to discover things about himself and others. Reading a physical book now can be an act of everyday defiance.

Too much ink and too many pixels have already been wasted lamenting the death of the book. In fact, sales reports from early 2017 show that print publishing has increased for the third year in a row (Segura).[2] More books are being printed each year, but that alone shouldn't offer us solace. The loss of books is less important than the loss of the bookish. As the photographs in *Codex* illustrate, the loss of books is natural, even when it is tragic. With enough time, everything will become trash.

The bookish need not respond to this upheaval with blanket technophobia. Critics since Socrates have worried about the relationship of writing, distraction, and memory. Digital information technology and e-books have, not surprisingly, only inflamed these anxieties. But look at the history of the book, and one cannot miss the fact that written communication has often been at the forefront of cultural, technological, and economic change. Indeed, we wouldn't have access to plentiful, cheap, and long-lasting paper books without generations of exactly these kinds of disruptive changes. When we ask why people no longer bother to read like they once did, we should blame a culture that polices our productivity, not new technology.

Labor experts rightly worry that Americans work far more than any other industrial nation (Rosen).[3] The

2. Segura, Jonathan. "Print Book Sales Rose Again in 2016." *Publishers Weekly.* 6 Jan. 2017. 20 May 2017. https://www.publishersweekly.com/pw/by-topic/industry-news/bookselling/article/72450-print-book-sales-rose-again-in-2016.html

3. Rosen, David. "Americans Work Too Long for Too Little." *Counterpunch.* 24 June 2016. Accessed 20 May 2017. http://www.counterpunch.org/2016/06/24/americans-work-too-long-for-too-little/

truly noxious effect of all this extra worktime, I'd argue, is the heightened expectation of *pure* pleasure and *utter* relaxation during leisure time. Reading is work. And when one works many hours at their job(s), is it no surprise that they are reluctant to put in additional time working through a complicated piece of non-fiction or a long novel rather than turn to less strenuous forms of entertainment and erudition.

One of the big reasons that the book and, more specifically, the novel, became so popular was to try and meet a burgeoning middle-class's demand for interesting ways to spend their newfound leisure time. The renowned historian of the novel Ian Watt goes as far as to attribute the rise of the novel in the eighteenth century to the rise of the modern conception of "the individual," each with her own personal dreams, desires, and preferences.[4] Novels offered a model of individual consciousness that, in turn, could be consumed by similar, albeit separate, conscious individuals. These novels were marketed to those already lucky enough to have time to themselves. The novel format sold so well because it gave people new ways to make sense of themselves.

Many digital reading technologies impede on the novel's traditional invitation towards solitary reflection. These devices are marketed as making our lives easier and more efficient, but much of that eases comes by requiring us to contribute our own labor, ingenuity, and cognitive surplus. We are not compensated for sharing things on social media, for example, but we put in hours managing these profiles all the same. From this perspective, the complaint that reading a book is *too much work* starts to come unhinged. In post-industrial Western society, nearly all people have at least some unscheduled time. Far more people have this kind of time than during the rise of the novel, but today, digital

---

4. Watt, Ian. *The Rise of the Novel*. Berkeley: U of California P. 2001.

devices often find a way to claim that time. The bookish need to find a way to take it back.

Each year, the University of North Dakota hosts a writer's conference. A few years ago, the conference's theme was "The Art of Science," an interdisciplinary topic aimed to attract the broader university and intellectual community. Featured writers are generally introduced by a faculty member or a university administrator. Milling around the book table after one of these readings, I overheard the person who had just introduced the writer, a person of considerable clout at the university, slough off buying a copy of the visiting writer's book. "Who's got the time?" he asked a woman I took to be his wife.

This excuse saddens me. If a well-heeled university professional doesn't have enough leisure time to read, who does? How can we writers, educators, students, and readers expect to convince the public about the value of ideas as even the most secure among us wither under the ever-tightening pinch of productivity? First, we need to stop idealizing work for work's sake. Leisure time should not be thought of as just a chance to indulge our guilty pleasures, but as time we get to work on *the self* and not for the boss. Reading promotes the kind of self-fashioning and self-education which has brought us to where we are as a civilization. Books are uniquely designed to teach us many of these skills, all the while reminding us of all that we don't, and maybe, can't, ever know. And that's where the imagination comes in. Good books don't offer easy answers, but reading can still offer camaraderie in a time of nihilism and despair. More than just stimulate the exploration of the self, books also propose an imagined community of other readers. There are all kinds of bookish people out there. We can find them within the pages of a book.

My experience at that recent conference reminds me of the Blue Scholars, a Seattle hip-hop duo. Their track "Southside Revival," a protest song written in response to the original election of George W. Bush, perfectly sums up the busy person's false opposition. Their emcee raps: "You say there's no time to study, people look. If you've got time to take a shit, you've got time to a read a book."[5]

Word.

The bookish must find a way to emphasize the benefits of technological change above and beyond personal convenience. We have access to more books and more ideas than ever before, but this surfeit can also work against our engagement with them. In response, the bookish must discover better ways to publicize the personal and social rewards of reading. To be bookish today means not to idealize the physical book itself, but to fight for reading in all its forms and formats. If we care about books today, we cannot afford to repeat wisdom worthy of the wall of an elementary school classroom. Look at Bloom's photographs of codices that comprise *Codex* and one can't help but start imagining a more compelling defense of the book as a thing worth saving.

---

5. Blue Scholars. "Southside Revival." *The Long March EP.* Massline. 2004.

Four Parts Water
Justin Sorensen

A man's life was totally dependent upon the
same microscopic events that would eventually
destroy his life and return him to dust.

– Lois Phillips Hudson, *The Bones of Plenty*[1]

I.

A few years ago I dreamt that I was crossing a stream with a man at
dusk. I don't remember where we were, only that we were carrying
all of my books. Gradually the water started to rise until it reached
our waists. As we were halfway across, I tripped and dropped my
share into the water. I wanted to keep moving but the man said
we should stop and gather them up. He started to lift them out and
hand them back to me one by one. I immediately saw that they
were all in perfect condition as though they had never fallen in. He
began to tell me how valuable they were and that I should never let
them go. I remember him giving me two books by _____ and a copy
of _____. I woke up weeping to see my books were still on the shelf
hanging over my head. I'm not sure if we ever made it across.

1. Lois Phillips Hudson. *The Bones of Plenty.* (Boston: Little Brown and Co.
1962) 195.

II.

I can't remember what the couch looked like. It might have been gray or brown. It was on the right as you walked into the room, placed against the wall, facing an old TV and chair. The walls were a pale green and needed to be painted––they were starting to chip around the trim. The room felt dated and worn. I walked in and sat down on the edge of the couch. I was leaning forward with my elbows on my knees, a posture I tend to naturally assume. That day I had at least two reasons for sitting this way. On the one hand, I thought it would exhibit interest toward what was directly in front of me. I thought it would display a quiet excitement and curiosity. It also helped my back. But there was another angle to this posture, an angle I wanted to keep hidden; it kept me from getting too immersed into what I could not fully see. It made sure I was ready. And herein is the problem: I'm always ready to move, always thinking about the next step. It is extremely difficult for me to get comfortable and sit still, which was a lesson I needed to learn in that moment. Rather than being where I was, I was thinking about how I was going to leave. And rather than staying seated, I was thinking about how long I'd have to wait before I got up again. I don't actively seek this; I've fallen into this habit. What I did know was that directly behind my back was a cushion waiting to absorb my body. That cushion was an invitation to close the space between my back and the couch. Maybe that would've helped me to see what was in front of me, which was a man who understood what it meant to sit slouched in a chair.

To be completely present in something is a divine characteristic which marks the saints.[2]

2. Solrunn Nes. *The Mystical Language of Icons.* (Grand Rapids: Wm. B. Eerdmans Publishing Company, 2005) 20.

When I looked at that couch I began to think of all the dust, dirt, and sweat that passed through its fabric—of all that was kicked up once I sat down. All those particles spinning through space, passing through shafts of light. I often fail to remember how everything is being held in place. The last time this occurred to me was when I was driving through Arizona with my brother a few summers back. It was getting on evening and the sun was casting a warm, fuzzy glow across the land. We had been talking for the better part of an hour when suddenly we stopped. It gave me a chance to turn and stare out the window. As I was looking out at the desert I realized I could disappear; that the world was not waiting on me. It was like I woke up to see that things were happening the whole time. Cacti were scattered across the hills holding their place. I saw that I was just picking up where someone else left off, and that now it was my turn to carry this for a little ways before I handed it over. That's how it's always been. There've always been scorpions in the desert. I'm sure that couch has held a lot of weight, that its current form is the product of years of impressions bearing down into it. Even if they're not visible, they're still there. At the time I would've said I was just sitting, not doing anything. I certainly wasn't thinking about what was underneath me, about all those layers of history. How did they come to be? What gave them their shapes? What did they have to pass through before they found themselves on that couch? In that present moment, I wasn't thinking about any of that. Instead, I was offering my layer.

Where I was, sitting before him, I realized that I had nothing left to say. The GPS was back in my car. It had started me at one point that took me to another until I found myself in a room with no more steps to take. I was at a place that was beyond navigation, where all I could do was sit and study what was before me. I had to stop asking questions so that I could learn how to sit on that couch. But I couldn't do that. Because I was thinking about my car, and about getting home to another room with another couch, where I could sit at my own pace. What I couldn't see was that I was sitting on an object that was long enough to hold the length of my entire body, that it was a place to rest my head. I couldn't see that for five minutes it offered me time to pause before I got up again. And I couldn't see that during those five minutes that I was on that couch that a river near Manitoba slowly began to rise.

III.

In her essay "Reflections on the Right Use of School Studies with a View to the Love of God," Simone Weil writes: "Attention consists of suspending our thought, leaving it detached, empty, and ready to be penetrated by the object [...] Above all our thought should be empty, waiting, not seeking anything, but ready to receive in its naked truth the object that is to penetrate it."[3] This essay is about learning how to pray. At its core, prayer is a matter of cultivating one's attention. Attention is a way of being receptive to what is in front of us by helping us to become aware of what is in front of us. This begins, first of all, by not imposing oneself onto an object, but by allowing the object to form an impression onto the student. This requires suspending one's assumptions about what an object should be, so that it may reveal itself as it is. Enabling this requires the removal of one's prejudices in order to properly receive what is being offered. For Weil, our studies are not about what we naturally gravitate toward; study is not about developing one particular area of interest. Rather, all subjects, regardless of our performance, provide an opportunity to learn how to pray. However, we need to enter into our studies with the right desire. This means that we

3. Simone Weil. *Waiting for God.* (New York: Harper Perennial Modern Classics, 2009) 62.

need to see study as an act of counter-formation, bending us back into the Image of God. This will allow us to see facets of the divine that we may have closed ourselves off to. Attention is crucial when viewing the film *Codex*. I want to propose that it's within the first ten minutes of the film that we are given an opportunity to develop this kind of attention.

Before a discussion of the film can begin, it's important to acknowledge the role of photography within *Codex*. *Codex* is, in fact, a multi-media project, combining installation, photography, and writing. The photographs serve to compliment the moving image, thereby extending the perspective offered by the film. They bracket moments that are happening just outside the frame; they are sketching out the scope of this event. That being said, it would be a mistake to simply see them as notation - marks made within the margins of the film. They are a way of processing the totality of the flood, and therefore should be seen in their own light. It could be argued that they establish the framework without which it would be extremely difficult for the film to subsist. They give the film its form, while providing a space to rest that is not dictated by time. All that to say, it is crucial that the photographs be viewed in tandem with the film.

Throughout the first half of the film, you see fragments of various books spread across the landscape, having arrived there by way of a flood that devastated Minot, North Dakota. Initially there is no human interaction with these objects. Words are under water, and insects move across pages. Books are suspended from the trees and scattered across the ground. It quickly becomes evident that these books are out of place: they aren't supposed to be hanging from the trees. They should be on the shelf, not on the ground. The camera is aware of this and pays attention to it. Even though initially there is no human engagement captured within the frame, the viewer is being conditioned to learn how to view what she is being shown.

Traditionally, a book is meant to be held, to be read, marked and absorbed. And the books in this film may have been interacted with in these ways. However, they are being seen differently now. As a result, they have to be approached differently and handled in a way that is mindful of this new context. While particular words are framed at different points throughout the film, the context out of which these words have come has been so far removed that it becomes crucial to reconsider what we are seeing. Inevitably we will come with our own associations. We will begin to forge connections between what we are seeing on screen and the things we may have read or encountered. That isn't necessarily a wrong way to begin. However, these associations should be held loosely. *Codex* suggests, albeit quietly, for us to hold these associations back so that a deeper truth can emerge. This requires recognizing that, perhaps, it is not so much about what is being carried within the book (as important as that can be) so much as it is about how we move after we encounter it.

This is the significance of that first ten minutes. Within that time we see a collection of images that prepare us to move into the second half of the film. The camera goes in and out of focus. What initially appear to be the remnants of the flood are actually the surface where life has begun to act. It is here that the film allows us to look again at this devastation. Before moving on from it, it needs to be accepted. That means paying attention to what's happening within, to put the whole thing in perspective. This happens by observing, looking closely within each of those moments to see what is being offered: a bee pauses before taking off again, ants move along the surface of a page; a centipede crawls out of the frame as spiders dance across their webs. Life is still happening.

Another shot shows sunlight slowly moving across the ground lighting up the earth while a train passes by. Work wasn't called off. Trains are still headed to their destination. It's within this range of perspectives that *Codex* is training us to alter our requests. It's not about wanting things to return to the way they were before the flood. What we need to do is receive - accept - what we've inherited. This is the underlying proposal of the film. Even though things look differently now, maybe the course hasn't changed. Maybe this is how it was always intended to be. Maybe the flood was supposed to come so that we could see that there is a harmony that was never shaken, that keeps running, humming underneath it all. It won't do any good to resist, because life is still going to happen. That awareness can actually bring conciliation. Because what may have been perceived as an interruption actually helps us see that we are not at the center, but instead are circling around that center. Therefore, it's not about trying to construct our own narrative, as much as it's about participating in the one that's already happening.

Participation requires humility: a willingness to submit to an established order. This submission is a prerequisite to contribute anything lasting. "Instruction is meant to prepare us for what may come, but few instructors will admit that every forward inclination, even a life-enhancing one, is another step toward death."[4] No matter how much we may resist and push against the inevitable, we will ultimately be absorbed into a force that is much larger than any of our efforts. As the books slowly break down, the ideas carried within them will be measured by a higher order. Everything that contributes to the momentum that is already in place will be sustained, while everything else will be cast out.

---

4. Larry Woiwode. *A Step from Death: A Memoir.* (Berkley: Counterpoint, 2008) 156.

Weil writes that Attention does not come through seeking. It does not come by setting out because in setting out the student presumes to know where she is headed. Attention requires patience. It is not obtained by rushing into understanding, for in doing so it's possible that the student may miss understanding entirely. No, attention happens through immersion, through submission. It is an effort that does not depend upon our understanding, so much as it depends upon our willingness to submit to what is before us. *Codex* shows us images of a flood that washed over a town leaving books scattered across the earth. Moving forward requires the acceptance of this, which will mean letting those first ten minutes of the film unfold. Of course, Weil was speaking of prayer, which is not primarily about making requests. It is sometimes that, but more importantly, it is about learning to be at rest in the acceptance of what we cannot control. It is about recognizing that we have entered into a story with objects. To understand these objects - to see *them* and not our *idea* of them - we need to get out of the way. It is then, and only then, that we can see what's before us. That's what the insects are showing us and what the waters revealed: how the books are now to be read.

IV.

(There is a parable in the Bible about two men out in a field. It's a parable I've been thinking about for my entire life. Two men out in a field when the Son of Man comes back. One of them is taken and the other is left. I always wondered what that man thought when he saw that he was alone - *what would he do?* Would he keep working or would he look to see who else was left? I've often wondered what man I would be. If I heard the prophecy right, if I'd be taken up or if I'd be left behind. When I was a child, I thought I wanted to be lifted up until I saw that I was reading those words all wrong. Noah built a boat that carried every animal in it, two by two. For forty days waters came and covered the earth. God spoke to Noah so he knew that that flood was coming. He knew that everyone was going to be taken, that only he was going to be left. I don't know what he thought when he was given those words, when he saw those waters spread out before him like some ancient vision. I guess he just had to stay still, and wait for the moment when it would all get pulled back. How did he live with that when he saw what story he inherited? *How did he watch the water?*)

"Ribbit," said the Frog.
"What's up," said the Man:
The Double Blind Redemption
in Micah Bloom's Codex
Robert E. Kibler

Humanity and the natural world: a reality shared by two exclusive entities, the one separate, brooding, thinking, creating, wondering and intuitionally afraid; the other comprehensive, inclusive, transformative and instinctively whole. To each, presumably, the other remains at once mysterious and somehow kin. For our part, we recognize the relationship, and desire it, for in the guise of the other we sense something of the self. But whatever we share dwarfs in comparison to the ineffable difference there is between us— or between me, let's say, and the swooning frog at home in the weedy bog. We are alien, different. It is a difference of scope as wide as it is long, and its length forever, humbling us by the contrast. This fascination of the self within the *other*, as much tendered by recognition as it is inhibited by alienation, results in a need to somehow redeem the self through seizing its essence, partly recognizable in the other, though we can only know a thing from our own perspective, so fall short, always. This failed attempt to understand the other through the lens of the self lies at the heart of Micah Bloom's film about work, respect, and redemption; *Codex*.

Bloom's short film consists of a mixture of stills and moving shots, underwritten by singular piano or cello accompaniment which aids and abets the emotional quality of the images, shots taken of books lost to the world of humankind as a result of the massive flood in Minot, North Dakota, in 2011. It is a powerful film whose lens views nature both up close and from far away, the micro of the biologist, the macro of the person seeking god. Broken into a prologue and six chapters, images of books sodden in nature appear in creeks, trees, by railroad tracks, amid the natural world of wooded ponds full of duckweed, cold running creeks, frogs, insects, ladybugs, wasps, walking ants, millipedes, butterflies, and spiders moving about their webs, or still, waiting in the quiet. The landscape of lost books, unnaturally strewn about the natural world, doubtless serves as emblem of human civilization, itself built on words, ordered, remembered, separate, whole. What has the word to do with this wild nature? More, perhaps, when settled in the muck. Books often appear in the film as alien things transformed by wind and water into blossomed grey bouquets here, there, and everywhere. Bits show words, "her," or "I am," "blackforest," "hope." The words are clearly ours, us, while the floral bouquets suggest an essential pulp that perhaps never was.

Halfway through the film unspoken human workers suited in white and wearing blue latex gloves begin to collect the books, painstakingly, tenderly, wrapping each in a shroud of white paper. Then they are numbered, tagged, and brought to a laboratory full of lights, tables, bottles, graduated cylinders and more concealed silent workers in white. Eventually the tagged books are returned to nature for funeral rites. They are either interred in the earth by the slow and silent work of a man with a spade, or cast off into the waters as a burning pyre fit for Patroclus, Anchises, Dido, or Beowulf — all of whom likewise went up in sacred flames. And Peking man little more than four feet, ritualized flames, proffered to the unknown walking the earth 750,000 years before us, likewise sprinkled two lines of red ochre on either side of its sepulchered dead, signifying some belief in a world beyond, an invisible world to which incomprehension could simply offer the burial rites of red ochre. And we have always thus reached out to the unknown, that we may be the closer to it, know it somehow. And as we fear that which we do not understand, suspecting its power over us, worship begins at the end of our reach. It is a reach with many branches. The ancient Egyptian statues of the gods constitute part of it, as do the early Greek *kouroi*, created partly in our image and born of our desire for affinity with the powerful and the unknowable at work in us. But for all of that, the world beyond our ability to articulate it remains mostly alien, imagined in a beyond that we are tragically fated to never altogether know, even as we think we shall see it, if only we keep probing, measuring.

The Scotsman Richard of St. Victor in the twelfth century asks us to view birds if we are to understand the nature of unseen things, and Bloom has offered us the same opportunity through sodden books—hybrid things, once of our world but reinvested in that of nature. Our world, as Bloom depicts it, is one of order, inspection, sanitation, and the machination of bright lights and fast clanking trains. Our camera lens surveys nature as does a biologist, and the workers in hygienic blue and suits of white, their well-lit labs, their careful tending of specimen books all show us what we fully know about ourselves. We observe from without, always searching, numbering, ordering. We do this even if by disposition, perhaps, we remain disinclined to actually touch what we measure, actually handle the unknown directly. We are the sorcerer's apprentice with an inner check telling us not to dabble in masterful things beyond our ken. But oh how we yearn to know, so we cannot help but seek the measure of things unknown yet ubiquitous. Accordingly, Bloom shows one observing worker at his task, sitting down, staring at a sodden book, attempting to read the inscrutable thing of nature it has become. Likewise, the various insects traversing the sunken pages appear equally outside of the words over which they walk, oblivious to the civilization those words represent. Bloom takes pains to show insects consuming bits of paper, covered with the detritus of decaying book, walking the pages of texts, mimicking the act of reading the language beneath their feet. Yet they deem nothing so important as to warrant a pause, so on they traipse, oblivious to us as we to them. Perhaps it speaks to the supremacy of instinct that nature turns or settles as it must, while we intuitively move, measure, quantify, do—or become worn down by settled oblivion, even as it is our fate to eventually be worn down anyway. Nature prevails, transforming our words, our lives, everything we know and value and remember into nothing so much as uncatalogued fodder for the bugs, while for it we perform our work and our sacred rites, rites full of questions, fear, homage, respect, and hope.

Herein lies the tale of *Codex*. We sense in nature the same forces that brought *Oxymandias*, Shelley's king of kings, to nothing but loss and anonymity amid the timeless swirl of desert sands, and we seek to understand those forces, perhaps control, subdue them. And while we often gain something for our efforts, inevitably we fail, concluding our search in homage to that which we do not know, performing our sacred rites of burial as if to signal a humility and respect at the end of our ordered reach. Doing so redeems the failure of our effort in the same way that fighting the good battle and raising the white flag redeems the lost enterprise of war. Likewise, the world of nature redeems itself through the well-wall of its own oblivion, for were its actions to occur as the result of sentience, we would suffer in our wearing down as victims of a cruel and mocking fate. Perhaps we do. Yet Bloom suggests that nature does not know its actions any more than we can control our own, so the bond between us remains. It is the bond of double-blind intention, immersed together in enigma, yet working all the same. It seems we have no means for knowing but a little of one another, and that according to our own terms—us with our tools of safety and measure, and nature alive in its inscrutable decompositing crawl. An impasse, wherein the frog blurts out "ribbit," and we answer with a "what's up," thus paying homage both to ourselves and to the familiar strangeness surrounding us, pregnant as it is with the bright flames of our pyre, at once truce, homage, and quest, ever turning its shine upon the dumb working movements of eternal night.

**Books as Bodies:
A Meditation on Micah Bloom's
Codex as Memento Mori**
Ryan Stander

*All those young photographers who are at work in the
world, determined upon the capture of actuality,
do not know that they are the agents of death.*[1]

– Roland Barthes

Keep death daily before one's eyes.[2]

– St. Benedict

American writer Susan Sontag once suggested, "Photography is an elegiac art, a twilight art. Most subjects photographed are, just by being photographed, touched by pathos."[3] Micah Bloom's *Codex* project traffics in such pathos. His images are an elegy to the 2011 flood that ravaged Minot, North Dakota. The exact details of how these books became strewn across a significant swath of the city is largely unknown. Where did they come from? Who did they belong to? In many ways, these questions are trivial to Minotians, or any other flood victims, who have faced so much debris passing in and under the turbulent stream. Objects pass by, become lodged in the residual muck, get covered in mildew and mold, and are eventually hauled to the curb for disposal. But is *Codex* primarily about books as flood debris or are there other shades milling around?

1. Roland Barthes. *Camera Lucida: Reflections on Photography* (New York: Hill and Wang, 1980), 92.

2. The Rule of St. Benedict, 4.47. *Western Asceticism.* Library of Christian Classics, Vol. XII. Ed. Owen Chadwick. Philadelphia: Westminster Press, 1958) 298.

3. Sontag. *On Photography.* (New York: Picador - Farrar, Straus and Giroux, 1973), 15.

Interpretation of any text is difficult because it always contains contextual elements partially localized in human experience, history, and culture. Photography further complicates interpretation. With painting or sculpture, viewers more readily recognize the distinct hand or style of the artist. However, in the face of all the factual information that photographs provide, viewers often forget the subjective vision of photographer and their role in making the image. As a result, most photographs live in the veracity of their surface record. In the digital world, "everyone is a literalist"[4] and tends to accept photographs as unmediated evidence, or "on the spot eye witness accounts" of reality.[5]

Questioning photographs and our relationship to them is essential. What are Bloom's intentions with *Codex*? Are his photographs a straightforward, documentary project? Are they symbolic, pointing toward some other idea? Or, could *Codex* exist somewhere in between? How the viewer answers these questions greatly shapes, or perhaps reflects, the interpretation.

Most people are likely to connect to *Codex* on the literal level as flood record. Bloom's photographs are captivating. They are filled with remarkable detail and other visual curiosities of insects and plants. Our eyes, trained by years of reading, scan the disintegrating texts for some recognizable words and memories. For those who lived through the flood in Minot, the visceral experiences are sure to shape their appreciation and interpretation of the work. Residents of Grand Forks, ND, or any other town which suffers floods, may approach the work slightly differently. It is still documentary flood material, but it becomes symbolic because it is not their flood. Through *Codex*, they recall their own brushes with Mother Nature, and this subtle shift opens the door for more imaginative readings.

4. Susan Sontag. *Regarding the Pain of Others*. (New York: Picador - Farrar, Straus and Giroux, 2003), 47.

Sontag argues that "any photograph has multiple meanings," and because they cannot speak for themselves, they are "inexhaustible invitations to deduction, speculation, and fantasy."[6] Bloom's work can certainly stand as a literal document to the effects of the flood. But those who stand outside the flood experience may sense other specters moving about. Bloom's work engages a difficult business of moving viewers' tendency for literal photographic interpretation toward a symbolic level. In his fine artist statement, Bloom refers to each book as a "unique soul." The artist himself thus imbues them with an anthropomorphic quality as human "bodies scattered across the streets, neglected in ditches... shamefully exposed, as if from a great disaster." They are scenes from a disaster or a great battle.

Elaine Scarry offers viewers a helpful insight on Bloom's move from the literal image to a metaphor of books as bodies. Scarry suggests that all human artifacts are intimately connected to their creators, regardless of size, type, or production means.[7] In them, we sense a human investiture, a distant fingerprint, flashes of human imagination and will. They are projections of their creators' mind and subsequently reciprocate the creators' values. It is here that we connect with the pathos of Bloom's flood debris. We see these objects strewn about, and imagine their once cherished status to both creator and owner. But Scarry, and I believe Bloom as well, push beyond this. Scarry suggests that we imagine or project not only the trace fingerprints of the objects' creator, but we instill the object with human forms and capacities. Bandages and

---

5. Laurie Cassidy. "Picturing Suffering: The Moral Dilemma in Gazing at Photographs of Human Anguish" in *She Who Imagines: Feminist Theological Aesthetics.* Ed. Laurie Cassidy and Maureen H. O'Connell. (Collegeville, MN: Liturgical Press, 2012), 103.

6. Sontag. *On Photography*, 23.

7. Elaine Scarry. *The Body in Pain: The Making and Unmaking of the World.* (New York: Oxford University Press, 1985), 280.

clothes represent human skin. Eyeglasses, microscopes, and cameras are symbolic equivalents of the human eye.[8] While bandages as skin and cameras as eyes are more graphically obvious, humanity also connects objects to various bodily capacities. Photographs, films, and books express the human spirit and capacity for memory.[9]

It is our imagination as viewers that allows us to see "this" as "that", books as bodies. Bloom's books are not the pristine texts we encounter in bookstores or libraries. They are not book as "idealized models" of fashion or product photography. They are book as "corpse." They are splayed open, missing limbs, gashed and torn. Their knowledge and memories have spilled out and are slowly soaking into the soil.

Nothing in the history of photography has been left beyond the camera's purview, including death and horrible acts of violence. Bloom's move toward metaphor of "book as body" opens a line of inquiry running through both documentary and art photography relating to images of death.[10] While many viewers may be morally reticent or simply squeamish about images of suffering and death, many such images still exist in our collective memory and visual culture.

Viewers may have first encountered death in photography through Hippolyte Bayard's staged 1840 *Self Portrait as a Drowned Man*.[11] Bayard's photo shows him, propped up, in a studio which points to another nineteenth century practice of post-mortem photography. When life

---

8. Scarry, 282.
9. Scarry, 283.
10. Each genre, here documentary and art photography, raises its own sets of important questions, most of which are well beyond the scope of this essay. However, Laurie Cassidy's article, noted above, helps navigate some of the interpretive issues at stake in terms of the spectator and spectacle, "the gaze", and embedded power relationships related to documentary photography.

expectancy was much shorter and rates of infant mortality were much higher, studios would often stage family photographs with the deceased. Through artifice of posing and arrangements, families could stage the photograph they hadn't captured during the person's life.

As the role of photography changed in society, it was drawn into mass communication. With the onset of the Crimean War, British photographer Roger Fenton was the first to extensively document war. While his wet plate collodion process was too slow to capture the fast action of battle, Fenton documented its aftermath but avoided photographing the injured and dead. Such scenes were left to the viewers' imagination. His well-known image *The Valley of the Shadow of Death* shows a sloping road, gently rising to the horizon from right to left leading the viewers' eyes through the landscape littered with cannonballs.[12] Its lowered position among the hills leaves the viewer with a certain amount of fear as they imagine the cannonballs flying in from unseen combatants.

But it is the American Civil War and Matthew Brady's coterie of photographers that brought the horrors of war to the general public. At the time of the war, Brady ran a successful portrait studio in Washington D.C. and gathered teams of photographers, each equipped with darkroom wagons allowing mobile access to Union encampments near battle lines. Some of the most well-known photographs of the war were produced by Brady's photographers Timothy O'Sullivan and Alexander Gardner. O'Sullivan's *A Harvest of Death* from Gettysburg in 1863 shows a sprawling atmospheric landscape littered with dead soldiers through the fore and mid-grounds.[13] Gardner's *Home of a Rebel Sharpshooter* and

---

11. https://commons.wikimedia.org/wiki/File:Hippolyte_Bayard_-_Drowned
     man_1840.jpg#/media/File:Hippolyte_Bayard_-_Drownedman_1840.jpg
12. http://www.loc.gov/pictures/item/2001698869/
13. http://www.loc.gov/pictures/item/2006685384/

Execution of the Lincoln Conspirators present unflinching records of the war.[14]

Photographic technology continued to evolve with faster lenses and films allowing more photographers to enter the battles themselves. Robert Capa's *Death of a Loyalist Militiaman* from 1936 captures the instant of a soldier's death by a sniper's bullet in the Spanish Civil War. With an arm outstretched toward the edge of the frame, the body crumples backwards down toward his grave-like shadow. World War II gave us harrowing photographs of human shadows burned into brick by atomic blasts and horrific records of the Allies' liberation of the Nazi concentration camps. The Vietnam era brought many more violent images of death into the collective memory from Malcom Brown's image of Vietnamese Mahayana Buddhist monk Thích Quang Duc's self-immolation (1963),[15] Eddie Adam's brutal image of *South Vietnam National Police Chief Nguyen Ngoc Loan Executes a Suspected VietCong Member* (1968),[16] John Paul Filo's moving photographs at the Kent State shootings (1970),[17] and Ronald Haeberle image of the My Lai Massacre showing deliberate civilian casualties (1968) later turned into the infamous *Q. And babies?* (1970) anti-war poster by the Art Worker's Coalition.[18]

This brief historical survey highlights both the extent of natural and human-inflicted violence as well as our constant documentation of it.[19] Many of these photographs have risen

---

14. https://www.loc.gov/item/cwp2003000205/PP/
    https://www.loc.gov/item/2010648748/
15. https://web-beta.archive.org/web/20170216183008/
    http://rarehistoricalphotos.com/the-burning-monk-1963/
16. https://web-beta.archive.org/web/20170217090014/
    http://rarehistoricalphotos.com/saigon-execution-1968/
17. https://www.loc.gov/item/2009632261/
18. https://www.moma.org/collection/works/7272
19. Anne Wilkes Tucker and Will Michels. *War/Photography: Images of Armed Conflict and Its Aftermath* is the new standard for a survey of war photography. (New Haven: The Museum of Fine Arts – Houston, 2012).

to the status of fine art and reside within museum collections because of their contribution to our collective consciousness. And yet, death and photography is not germane only to documentary and reportage. Contemporary artists like Sally Mann and Joel Peter-Witkin have both used corpses in their work (albeit in drastically different approaches).

American photographer Sally Mann's work stands as an interesting conversation partner with Bloom's *Codex*. Widely known for her large format photographs of her family and southern landscapes, she also has a long-standing fascination with death. Mann's book and film, *What Remains* offers remarkable images of her prized greyhound after its death and decay, landscape images where an escaped convict was shot on her property, and likely most disturbing, photographs of decaying human bodies at forensic research facility.[20] Connecting to the overarching theme, Mann also returned to Civil War battlefields from Fredericksburg, Virginia to Antietam, Maryland wondering:[21] what happens to the land when there are massive amounts of death on it? Does the land offer some form of witness to this history? To pursue these questions, Mann hauled her large format camera and wet plate collodion darkroom into those once again verdant fields. Mann reaches across time, dragging the viewers' imagination with her. Unlike the Civil War photographers, who prided themselves on objectivity and craft,[22] Mann's battlefield images are somber, dark and mysterious. They are idiosyncratic, filled with serendipitous imperfections that help viewers loosen their grip on the fact-filled present and re-imagine the experience, history, and place.

20. Sally Mann. *What Remains.* (Boston: Bullfinch Press, 2003).
21. https://web-beta.archive.org/web/20170101131946/
    http://sallymann.com/selected-works/battlefields
22. Naomi Rosenblum. *A World History of Photography*, Fourth Edition. (New York: Abbeville Press Publishers, 2007) 186. Many would contest the claim of objectivity, but not the aspect of craft in the work.

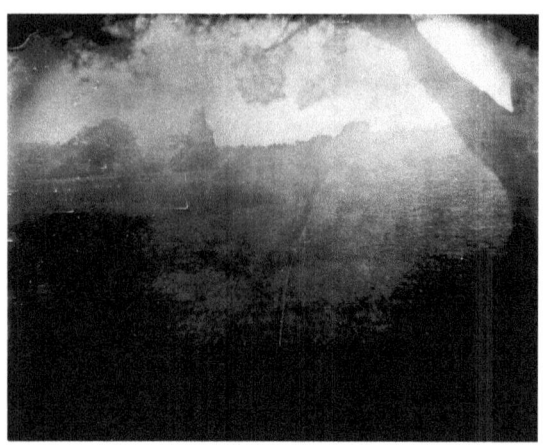

Sally Mann
Battlefield, Untitled, Antietam (Blast),
2001, gelatin silver print,
38 x 48 inches, (96.5 x 121.9 cm)
Edition of 5, Gagosian Gallery
© Sally Mann. Courtesy Gagosian.

While Bloom and Mann's work is visually distinct (Bloom's digital versus Mann's wet-collodion, color versus black and white, factual versus romantic), their work resonates deeply with one another. Bloom's images of books as bodies scattered across the landscape resides somewhere between Mann's Civil War landscapes and the images of bodies in the forensic facility. In spite of their visual differences, both artists help the viewer to consider death through an evocative, roundabout approach.

However, addressing photographs in terms of image content is only one way in which photographs need to be considered. Bloom's photographs are no different. Photography's veracity offers viewers a mediated record of facts and details of specific historical moments, including images of suffering and death. And yet, photography's most influential commentators have suggested that it has other, less obvious, but poignant relationships with death that exist outside of the image content.

Sontag pushes beyond the image surface toward a theory of photography that deals in life and death, suggesting, "after the event has ended, the picture will still exist, conferring on the event a kind of immortality."[23] "Photographs turn the present into the past" by stopping time.[24] For Sontag, "All photos are *memento mori*" meaning that they remind viewers of human mortality.[25] Sontag suggests, "To take a photograph is to participate in another person's (or thing's) mortality, vulnerability, mutability" because time continues to run.[26] Elsewhere, Sontag picks up that idea of time's stoppage, and life to a movie and photography to death.[27] "The click of the shutter is the moment of death. It converts the whole world into a cemetery. Photographers, connoisseurs of beauty, are also — wittingly or unwittingly — the recording-angels of death."[28]

Interestingly, Roland Barthes offers a similar comment on the role of the photographer. He writes: "All those young photographers who are at work in the world, determined upon the capture of actuality, do not know that they are the agents of death."[29] In their attempt to preserve and memorialize life, photographs produce a form of death.[30] More than Sontag, Barthes' seminal *Camera Lucida* teases out these obscure connections and draws our awareness, for better and worse, to the veracity of the photograph and its "evidential force."[31] For Barthes, each photograph is a

23. Sontag. *On Photography*, 11.
24. Susan Sontag. *Introduction to Portraits in Life and Death.* By Peter Hujar. (New York: Da Capo Press, 1976), Introduction.
25. Sontag. *On Photography*, 15.
26. Sontag. *On Photography*, 15.
27. Sontag. *Portraits*, Introduction.
28. Sontag. *Portraits*, Introduction.
29. Barthes, 92
30. Barthes, 92

"certificate of presence" and record of "what has been."[32] They exist as moments plucked from time and burned into silver and paper. It is, however, the lacerating slippage of time from the embalming moment of the shutter's click to our later attendance to the image that points toward death. This ever-widening gap between the shutter's stoppage and life's onward march always points toward our impending death. Whatever the photograph's subject, whether dead or alive, this reality exists and perpetually implicates each new viewer.

Several important questions remain. Whether literal or symbolic death and suffering, what are we as viewers to do with such images? How are we to "use" them? Or, as Sontag asks, "What good is served by seeing them?"[33] She is rightly concerned about culture's consumption of images, particularly those of violence. Can a "good" be brought about by images of death and violence? Can such images create or reinforce a moral impulse?[34] Ultimately, these questions relate back to issues of interpretation - "who" is looking at them?

What do Bloom's languishing books offer to humanity?

Codex traffics in both senses of photographic death explored above: one embedded in the content of the image surface and the other in the viewers' experience in looking. As

31. Barthes, 88
32. Barthes, 87, 93.
33. Sontag. *On Photography*, 20.
34. Sontag. *On Photography*,16-17.
   In terms of war photography and other images of suffering, Sontag is adamant that photographs of suffering cannot create the moral position, but they can reinforce an existing one and build a nascent one. She continues, "What determines the possibility of being affected morally by photographs is the existence of a relevant political consciousness. Sontag is not speaking of association with a particular political party. Rather politics in this sense suggests an outward commitment to ways of being a community.

flood record, Bloom's images function as historical prompts, helping viewers recall their own experiences with Mother Nature. The detail and pathos of these images may well inspire a sense of awe and curiosity in the natural processes, as well as a deepened compassion for victims of floods or other natural disasters.

As in Sontag's or Barthes' stoppages of time, *Codex*'s symbolic images of death also offer viewers an opportunity to meditate on their own existential condition. In them, we sense that in the midst of life, we are in death.[35] Humanity is haunted by this paradox. Our culture's tendency, says Sally Mann, is to avoid death, keeping it at arm's length. While Mann does not say it explicitly, her *What Remains* series functions as a prophetic mirror to culture. The same follows for *Codex*. With the force only a photograph can muster, Bloom and Mann remind us of our own impending death. It is precisely here that these and other photographs acquire their status memento mori. Whether or not Bloom's images inspire a changed perspective on life and death is a matter of personal context. However, photographs as *memento mori,* are constant reminders pointing viewers toward their death.

In the end, it is evident that Bloom's work flourishes on multiple levels and interpretive schemas. *Codex*, for those devastated by the flood, likely awakens painful memories and fears about future floods. And yet for others, it may function as a final statement, an emotional closure to the experience. For still others, it opens important opportunities to meditate on our human mortality. Bloom's work is a testament to the power of art, the beautiful difficulty of interpretation, and the remarkable depth of photography.

---

35. *The Book of Common Prayer* (New York: Seabury Press, 1979), 492. The ancient liturgical phrase for this is *Media vita in morte sumus*, or, "in the midst of life, we are in death."

Micah Bloom's Books
Brian Prugh

QUAESTIO.

Why, after the flood, when Micah Bloom sees a book by the side of the road, suspended in a tree, or submerged in the river, does he feel the need to honor it with a proper burial? I do not ask this question psychologically; I am not interested in who Micah Bloom is that he feels this need, but in what the book is that it could inspire such a need. Can the book bear such treatment?

This is the question: what kind of thing is the book? It is an ontological question, and the answer to that question bears on how I read the project documented in this book. If the book is the same kind of thing as other man-made things like ball-point pens and candy wrappers, then *Codex* must be something of a joke. It must be playing with our rituals of mourning, because we do not reverently bury a ball-point pen or candy wrapper; we throw it away. If it is eventually buried, this is accidental. It would be better if it just disappeared.

With the passing of a candy wrapper or ball-point pen out of usability, there is nothing to mourn, because these objects exist for us exclusively in their use. Once the ball-point pen runs out of ink or the candy wrapper is empty, it goes into the trash, without compunction. But when a human being dies, we *owe* something to the body—we owe it a proper burial—because of the kind of thing a human being is.

The claim latent in *Codex* is that we owe something to the book's body because of the kind of thing that it is. The book does not matter for us exclusively in terms of use, like the ball-point pen or the candy wrapper. The book is a different kind of thing, a more human kind of thing. Again, the question is: what kind of thing is it? What sets the book apart? What makes it fitting for the book to receive last rites?

Note on the state of the research.

This essay proceeds in a series of positions. Each position reaches for something essential about the book and the act of reading. Each fails in some way. Together they gesture at what the book could be—at what, I hope, books aspire to be.

Having spent an inordinate amount of time reading books myself, this study inevitably involves a question about why I have devoted my time in this way. My life is bound up in books (and in visual art and music), so an account of the book is an account of a significant portion of my life.

This places a great deal of pressure on the book *qua* book. It is a pressure that, sometimes, the book cannot bear. More often, though, it is a pressure that I cannot bear. I know that I fail the books I've read. Failures themselves are telling, though. If a book can fail me, or if I can fail a book, this says something about the way that a book can matter. And the way that it matters reveals something about what the book is.

Most of these reflections apply equally to other works of art (paintings, films, music, a book of images like this) but the image of the decaying book is the starting point so "the book" remains the center of my investigation.

FIRST POSITION: THE IMMORTALITY OF THE BOOK

> *So long as men can breathe and eyes can see,*
> *So long lives this and this gives life to thee.*[1]

William Shakespeare, Sonnet XVIII

When I started searching for the joint that might separate books from other kinds of things, I began with the thought that the book is a print, a mechanical reproduction, the visible, readable impression of some more abstract thing—call it the Idea of the Book. This invocation of the abstract order of the book suggests that there is something special about that order that gives us a reason to preserve it in a physical book, or to translate it into another language and print it in another book.

For Walter Benjamin in "The Work of Art in the Age of Mechanical Reproduction," the power of mechanical reproduction of an image is the pre-servation of the real in it, a reality that gets obscured by the "aura" of singular images. The ability to be mechanically reproduced acts as a guarantee that there is something real in the image, which he opposes to the artificial value created by scarcity or singularity. There is a lesson here that applies to the book—even if the book was once reproduced by hand, it has always existed as something essentially reproducible. And as the reproducibility of the image is the mark of its authenticity for Benjamin, the ability of a book to be reproduced, and the fact of its reproduction, testifies that there is something real in the book.

To push the point in Platonic language, the thought is that the Idea of the Book holds some piece of Reality—the really real—that enters the world in the physical form of the book. This would call out the book as a special kind of thing, a

---

1. Shakespeare, William. "Sonnet XVII." *Shakespeare's Sonnets.* Edited by Katherine Duncan-Jones. *The Arden Shakespeare.* London: Methuen, 1997. p. 147.

thing with a "spiritual" component that transmits some of its power onto the material remains that have become, through the destruction of the flood, no longer able to carry that component.

It is an idealistic move, calling upon an Idea of the Book that stands behind the physical one, a pure abstract order that the book preserves, takes part in, but does not exhaust. I might say: the book carries a message, some essential communication, some missive from a remote and urgent source. It is in light of this vital communication that we honor the vessel that holds it. It is the duty of the book to carry the message. We mourn the lost book like we mourn the runner who died carrying his message to Marathon.

The problem is that there is an important difference between the book and the runner at Marathon: the runner at Marathon is mourned not for carrying the message but because he was human, he lived and he died. The book, in the emphasis of its existence as a reproduction, is just a piece of technology. It holds a code. And even if the writer is great enough to "give life to" a person into this code, the vessel that carries the code does not matter.

It is an imperfect analogy, because however poetically I might describe the way the copyists hold the keys to immortality, the Idea of the Book remains wholly abstract, cold and distant from the humanity of the experience of reading. The analogy weakens; the divinity evoked in Shakespeare's sonnet flattens as the book's function reduces to storage in binary code—something a computer can do!

SECOND POSITION: THE UTILITY OF THE BOOK

I made this little drawing that I thought about using as the basis for this essay—an image for what the book is, for what it does.

It is an image, too, for the work of art, for the piece of music, etc.

It begins with a circle. The circle represents the horizon—everything that can be seen from the point in the center. My horizon is the outer limit of what I can see. It is everything that I can see when I look around. In a very real way, it is my world. On the open ocean on a clear day, the curvature of the earth falls away from a circular horizon with a radius of forty miles. (fig. 1)

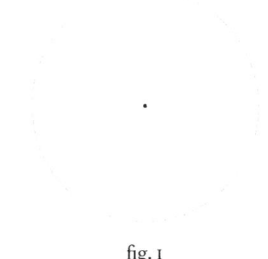

fig. 1

If this circle is projected onto a plane perpendicular to it, the resulting figure (H_l) is a line segment, equal to the diameter of the circle. (fig. 2)

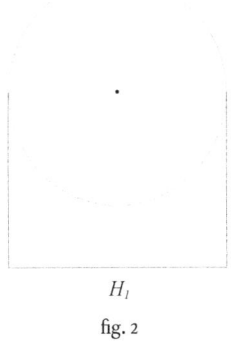

H_l

fig. 2

This is an image of the circle, viewed from the side. In the symbolic geometry of this figure, this image for my world, everything that I know, that I believe, and, most importantly, everything that is visible to me is contained in line segment H_1. (fig. 3)

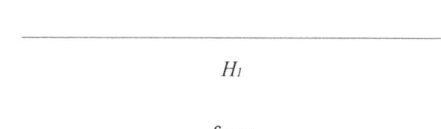

H_1

fig. 3

Those who have tried to draw what is in front of them know how very little of what is in front of them they actually see, how little is actually visible to them before they begin the drawing.

The next few steps create my first image of an encounter of my world with the book.

The book divides my world; it creates distinctions between things. I now see the world in different parts and pieces. There is structure that was not there before. I have names for things I might have long felt but never could articulate, that I never was sure were real. As an image for this, I divide H_1 into four equal segments. (fig. 4)

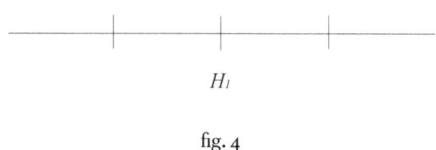

H_1

fig. 4

But the book also enlarges my world. I make connections between things that reveal a deeper reality hidden by the visible one.[2] My perception reaches beyond the flat plane that defines the horizon I have drawn. My image for this is to describe a circle through each endpoint of H_1, with H_1 as the

2. Baldwin, James. "The Creative Process." *The Price of the Ticket.* New York: St. Martin's / Marek, 1985. pp. 315-318.

radius. These circles meet above the center of the horizon—directly above the point that represents the place where I stand. (fig. 5)

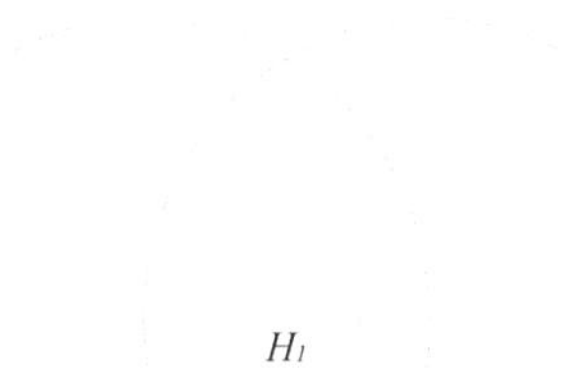

H_1

fig. 5

To describe the shape of what the book does, I extend lines from this point to the points that divide the horizon line. The resulting figure looks a bit like a mountain, with paths up to the summit. (fig. 6)

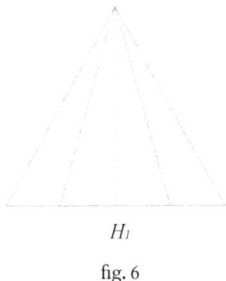

H_1

fig. 6

This seems fitting, for an encounter with a book can make a world rise around me like a mountain. It can spur me to reach after higher thing: Justice, for instance. Truth. Understanding. Virtue.

Martin Heidegger, in "The Origin of the Work of Art," claims that truth happens in the work of art (54).[3] One of Friedrich

3. Heidegger, Martin. "The Origin of the Work of Art." *Poetry, Language, Thought.* Translated by Albert Hofstadter. New York: Harper & Row, 1971. pp. 15-86.

Nietzsche's aphorisms in *The Gay Science* is a meditation on the book: "What good is a book that does not lead beyond all books?".[4] In my diagram, I create an illustration for the way that the book enlarges my world, allowing me to see the things in my world in new ways, from different heights. Once my world has been enlarged, once the truth has happened, once it is visible, I no longer need the book. It has led me beyond the book, if not all books. This is the utility of the book.

The consequence of this view is that, far from being an occasion for mourning, we should expect to see books littering the sides of roads, spilling out of the trash cans in subway stations, floating along rivers as they pass under bridges—that, in fact, this is their proper place, their owners having left them behind when they did not need them anymore—when they had gotten beyond the books.

THIRD POSITION: THE FINALITY OF THE BOOK

> *A lamp is on my table and the house is in the book.*
> *I will finally live in the house.*[5]

> –Edmund Jabès, *The Book of Questions*

Meyer Schapiro—deeply suspicious of Heidegger's political commitments—took him to task about his interpretation of a painting of shoes by Van Gogh that formed the interpretive center of "The Origin of the Work of Art." (This discussion between Heidegger and Schapiro figures prominently in Jacques Derrida's *The Truth in Painting*.)

The upshot of Schapiro's critique is that Heidegger makes Van Gogh's shoes mean what he *wants* them to mean— that a closer inspection of the painting reveals that the truth that Heidegger claims "happened" in the painting was less

4. Nietzsche, Friedrich. *Die Fröliche Wissenschaft.* Leipzig: Insel Verlag, 1982.
5. Jabès, Edmund. *Le Livre des Questions I.* Paris: Gallimard, 1965. pp. 22.

in the painting than in Heidegger. This is the danger of the view of the book set out exclusively in terms of the effect that it has in *my* life: I am in danger of losing sight of the book, or distorting the book, in the service of my own ends. I doubt Nietzsche or Heidegger fall easily into this pitfall, but the pitfall is there, and worth heeding.

While Schapiro's critique of Heidegger's reading of the painting does not necessarily undermine the deeper philosophical argument, it does carve out an important space beside the work that the book or work does on the reader and insists on its importance. For Schapiro, it isn't enough that Heidegger saw a painting of shoes by Van Gogh. He wants to know *what* painting of shoes he saw. Because, for Schapiro (and he's right here, it seems to me), the particulars of the painting matter for the truth that is available in it. There is no truth in the generic idea of a painting, only in the particular painting. And it is this insistence of returning to the painting, of returning to the book—picking it up, humbly judging that I might have been too hasty in having considered myself beyond it—that is the guiding force for the second half of this construction.

In my diagram, I draw another line segment (H_2) next to the mountain of the first. (fig. 7) Another line, another world. Jabès lives in the house that is the book: the book is a world he has made, it is the world he lives in. I draw another horizon next to the book in recognition of the fact that when I read the book, I meet another person. I encounter another world.

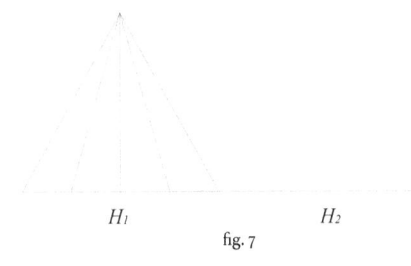

H_1 H_2

fig. 7

In a similar way I divide the horizon line next to my mountain. For the purposes of this diagram, I divide it into five segments: this world is divided differently than mine. (fig. 8) And in a like manner, I draw lines through the vertex of the equilateral triangle constructed on that line segment: I draw the mountain of the person standing beside me, the mountain of the person I encounter in the book. This image is now of two mountains, side by side, touching at a single point that is the book. (fig. 9)

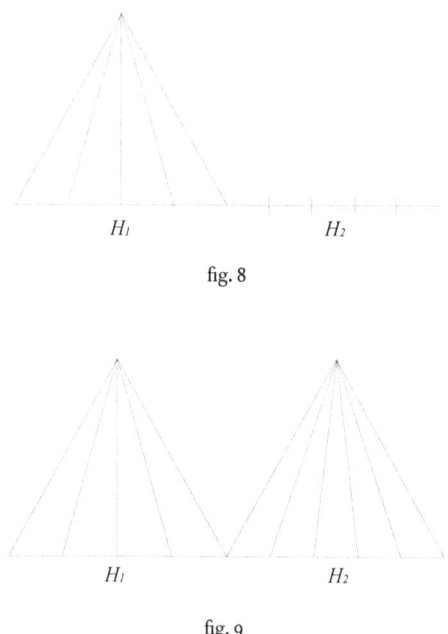

fig. 8

fig. 9

But this is a critical point, because at this point something unexpected happens. The problem with my diagram is that there is no obvious necessity to the next construction. It is an idea that I encountered while studying philosophy: the fusion of horizons.

The thought that I have taken away is that when there are certain kinds of encounters between people; whether through conversation, mutual action, a life together, through art or books, these two people, each of them living in their own worlds, meet, and their horizons merge so that they can look, together, out at a larger world.

The image in the diagram was to connect the peaks of the two mountains: to draw a new horizon created by the points outside of themselves formed by the peaks of their searching. (fig. 10)

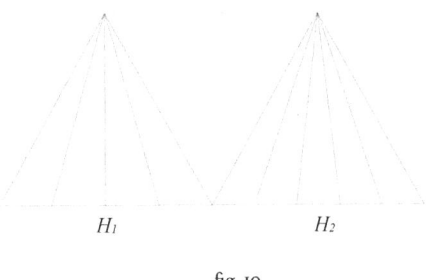

fig. 10

Having arrived at this image in my drawings I thought I was done. But there was still something wanting in the figure. So I drew lines connecting each mountain peak to each dividing point. (fig. 11) It gave the figure strength, stability. A two-point perspectival grid emerges between the peasks. And this visual effect symbolically knits the reader to the writer.

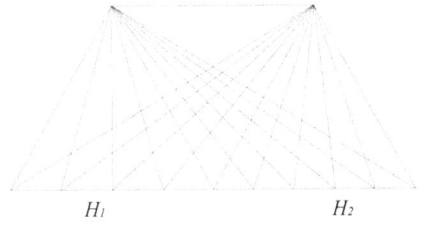

fig. 11

With these lines the drawing claims that the encounter widens that original horizon-line to encompass both worlds. And the figure is strong because the worlds have become enmeshed. One can no longer be pulled apart from the other. But here the book is not subsumed into the self of the reader. On the contrary, the reader and the book assume the stronger form only when they stand together.

(I make this claim with the works of "high art" that have shaped my life in mind, but the thought also applies to simpler things. Consider, for instance, a recipe for a meal. I read the recipe, and get an idea about how to prepare the meal. As I cook, I consult the recipe. I cook *with* the recipe. The recipe shapes my understanding of cooking, and I shape the recipe into my own meal. The meal comes from the recipe, but also from me. I prepare the meal, together with the recipe.)

This is my strongest case for the humanity of the book. And it is this image of the book that I would put forward as justification for Bloom's treatment of them. For the mystical power these lumps of plant fiber, glue, thread and ink hold for us. But doesn't this romanticize the book? Isn't it absurd in its implications?

FOURTH POSITION: THE ABSURDITY OF THE BOOK

This is a photograph of a climber who died on Mount Everest at 27,900 feet, about 1,100 feet below the summit. (fig. 12)

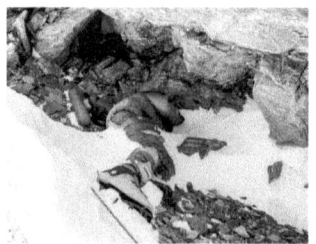

Figure 12.
Maxwellj040. Photo of "Green Boots," the Indian climber who died in 1996 on the Northeast Ridge of Mount Everest, 2010. Licensed under Creative Commons Share Alike 3.0 Unported license, https:/commons.wikimedia.org/wiki/File:Green_Boots.jpg.

fig. 12

It is one of many bodies on that giant mountain. Above a certain elevation, the removal of the bodies of the dead becomes practically impossible. More than one climber has died attempting to remove the remains of lost climbers, as Antigone gave up her life to bury her brother. The bodies are there, exposed to the elements like the books photographed in this volume.

There is something absurd about climbing mountains, and something of this absurdity touches my diagrams. There is no earthly reason to imagine I can see outside my horizon, or to imagine that the mountain that grows out of it is anything but a fiction. This charge is often leveled at the more bookish among us, that an obsession with these books (reading them, writing them, printing and preserving them) is selfish or unhealthy, that the "real world" demands our attention.

This absurdity sits in a strange way upon the climber pictured above. Climbing Mount Everest looks, from the outside, like an incredibly selfish act. Expensive, dangerous, and available as an experience only to those with incredible resources, it would appear to be the height of human folly, the pinnacle of Romantic longing.

Why climb the mountain? Did not the local people not have a greater reverence for the mountain by looking at the summit only from below? What is gained by looking at the base from above? Why climb when it has already been climbed? Why attempt what has already been done? What is to be gained in the repetition? Better to turn our attention to more pressing problems.

The evidence against this is this body: material proof that, at least to one person, it was worth dying for. To die on Everest is not the same as to die in a car accident, in a war, of disease, or fighting for justice. One need not intend to die to be killed in these ways: death is pressed upon the person by the force of necessity. (I must get home.) (The soldiers are approaching the city.) (I am mortal.) (Justice demands that I fight.)

We mourn these deaths in the usual ways: to the extent possible, we collect the remains. We clean them, present them at a funeral, and reverently lay them to rest. This is the normal course of events after a person's death. And the *Codex* team attempts to honor the material remains of books in these usual ways.

But by photographing them as they were found, Bloom subverts the usual order. He presents us with images that, when humans are involved, are usually filed away, out of public view (crime scene photographs, for instance). So we see the "bodies" out in the elements, like we see the body of the climber on Everest. Even if Bloom does go on to bury these books, the photographs leave them there. And their folly, in a way, becomes even more visible.

There is no necessity in climbing the mountain. Nothing demands the ascent. It is undertaken with the full knowledge that dying on the mountain is a possibility. The death is therefore gratuitous: this life is given freely. The body on the mountain reminds us of this. It questions, from above, the certainty of those who maintain the absurdity of such frivolous activities.

I read in the images of *Codex* a call to do more than mourn the loss of something that can live in the reader. I see a symbol for the book and the culture of books, for the absurd expedition ascending the steep face of that culture, for the danger of rendering it frivolous—I see in Micah Bloom's books the climber lost on Everest, out of reach of human recovery.

SED CONTRA.

If I understand the motive to bury these books, it is because I understand the need to bury the bodies left on Everest. But I must acknowledge that many of the families of those climbers have asked that the bodies of their loved ones remain on the mountain.[6] I acknowledge this because it speaks to something important about the relation of the climber to the mountain.

In an important way, those bodies belong to the mountain. Because climbers do not make the mountain a part of themselves, they become part of the mountain. Those who have climbed the mountain and have safely descended are part of the mountain. Those who remain are part of the mountain. And their bodies testify to this. And this testimony rejects the logic of the world, the utilitarian calculus, the pride of those who know that climbing mountains is stupid.

The book is made of trees, processed in water. It surely belongs to the earth, suspended in a tree, submerged in water, every bit as much as it belongs to its reader. But the book calls out from the river. It calls out from under the snow. It calls out from the rocks lining the railroad tracks.

It also testifies, but to what? I have attempted four times in this essay to articulate that testimony, but none succeeds. So what do I say, *on the contrary?*

Do I say (against the first position) that the reality of the book is not exhausted by the order of words preserved within its pages? Do I say (against the second position) that while I read books in order to grow, that the book is not exhausted in my growth? Or, further (against the third position), that it is not exhausted in the bonds of human community? Do I say (against the fourth position) that for all

---

6. Andrews, Travis M. "The extraordinary cost of removing dead bodies from Mount Everest." *The Washington Post.* 27 May 2016, www.washingtonpost.com/news/morning-mix/wp/2016/05/27/ the-extraordinary-cost-of-retrieving-dead-bodies-from-mount-everest/?utm_term=.baf87b179e48.

of its absurdity, the book is in fact *not* absurd, but a necessary and natural outgrowth of our being in the world?

But perhaps the true *sed contra* is not a claim, but an image. I do not yet know which image. Perhaps it is the fading light of the funeral pyre as it floats down the river. Or, perhaps, the book speaks more clearly in the very place where it does not belong, the place where it called out to Micah Bloom and began the project that became this book.

Codex

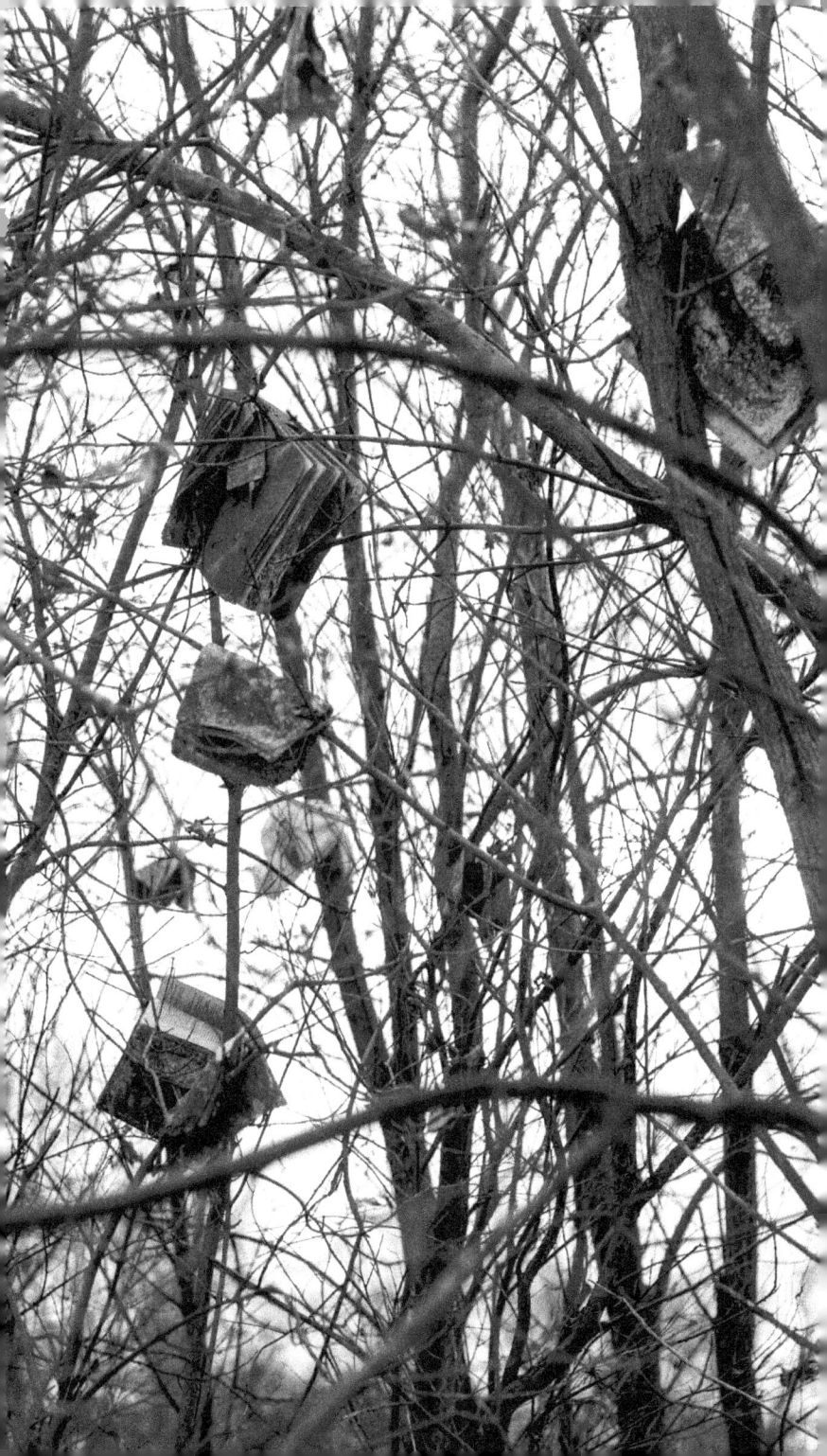

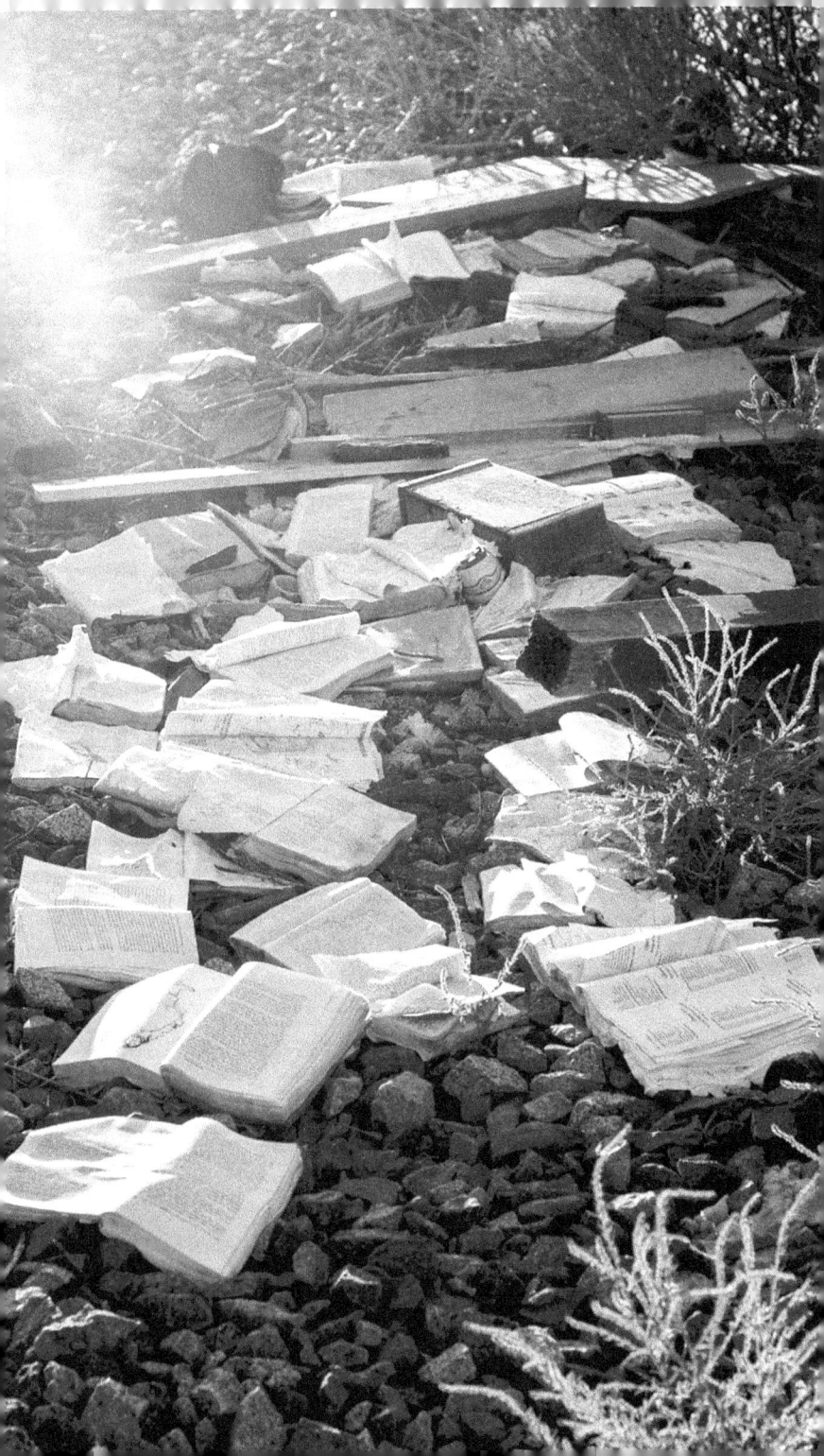

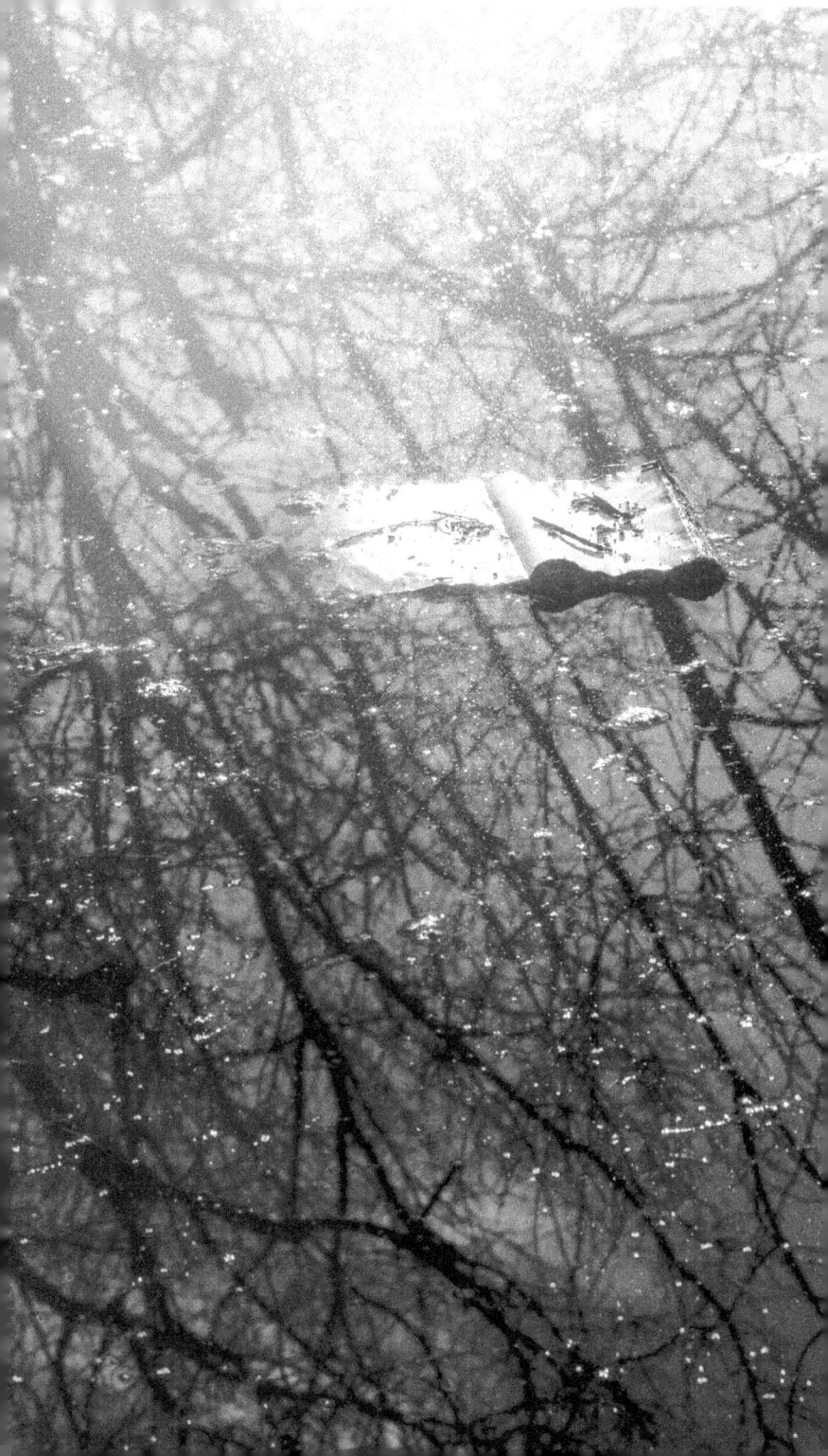

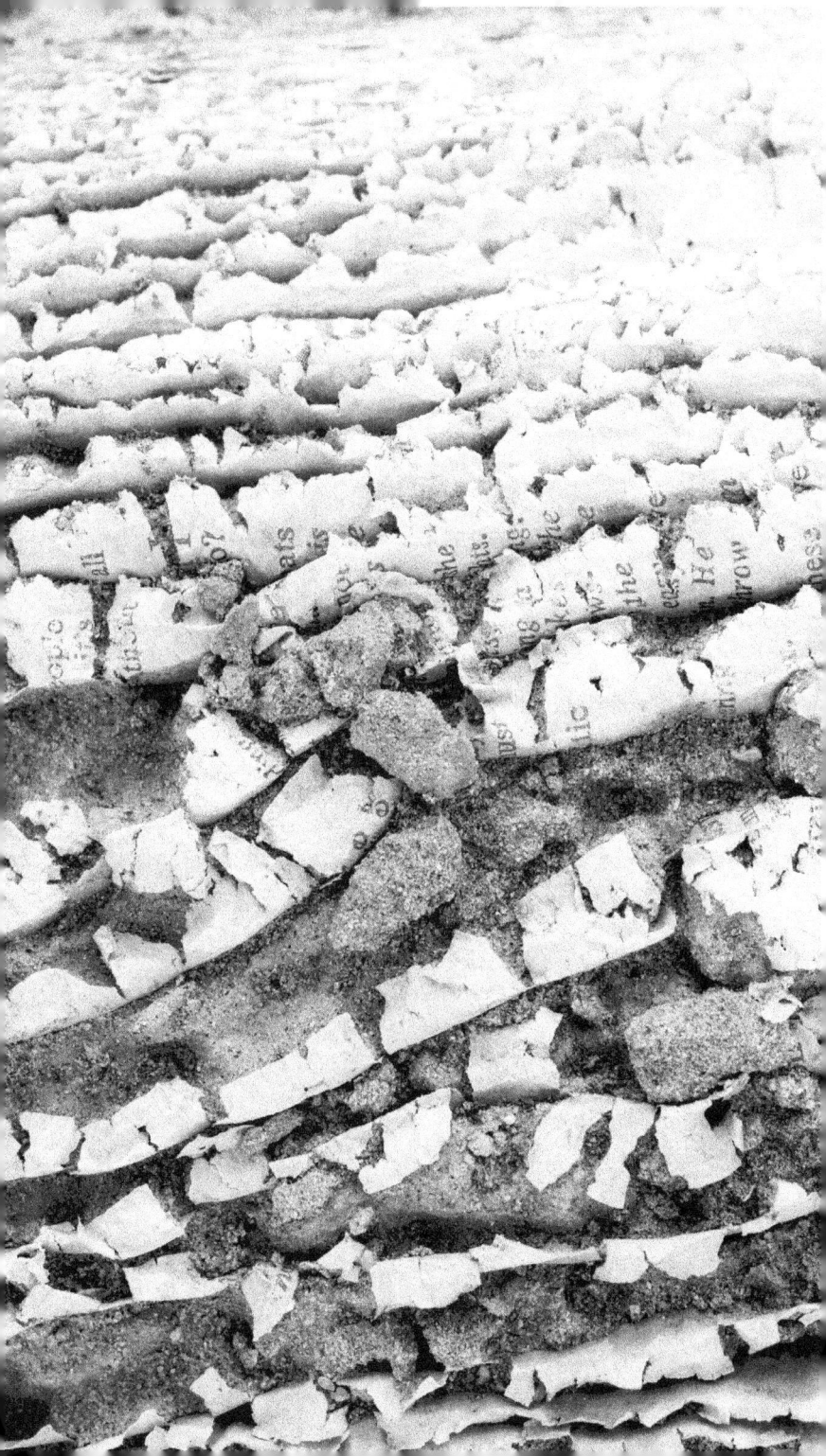

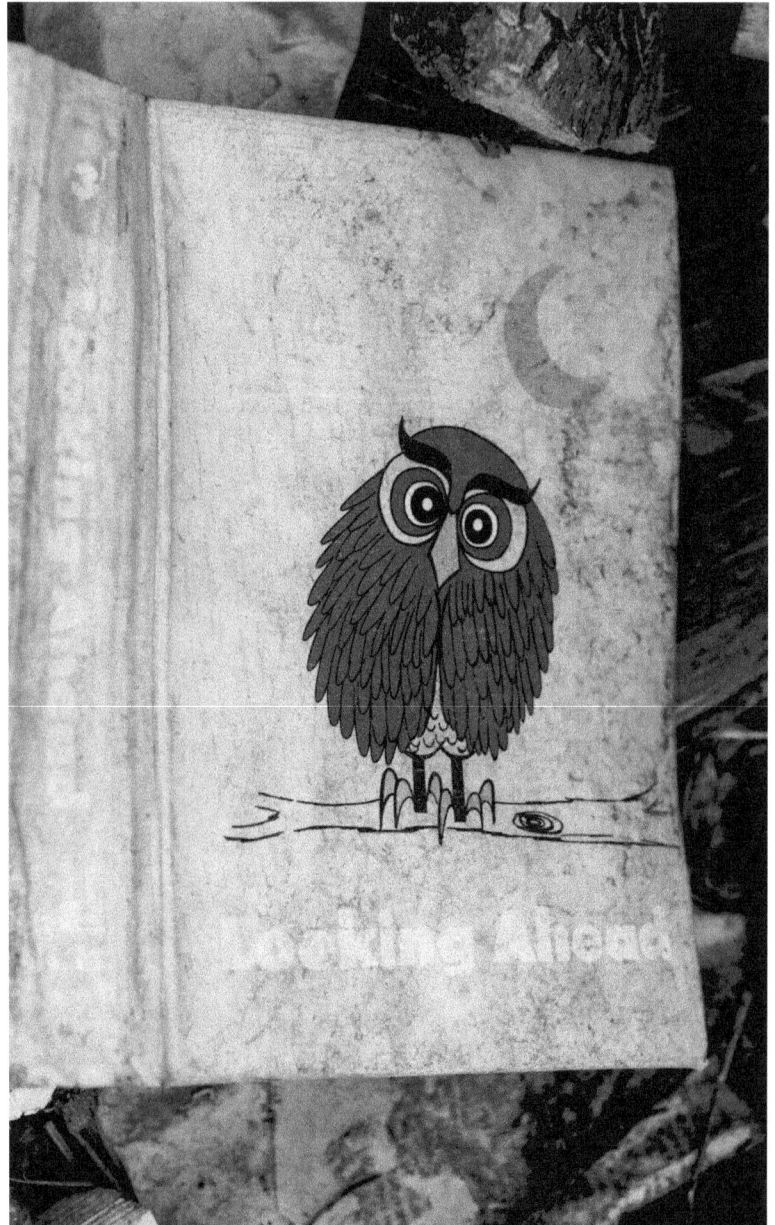

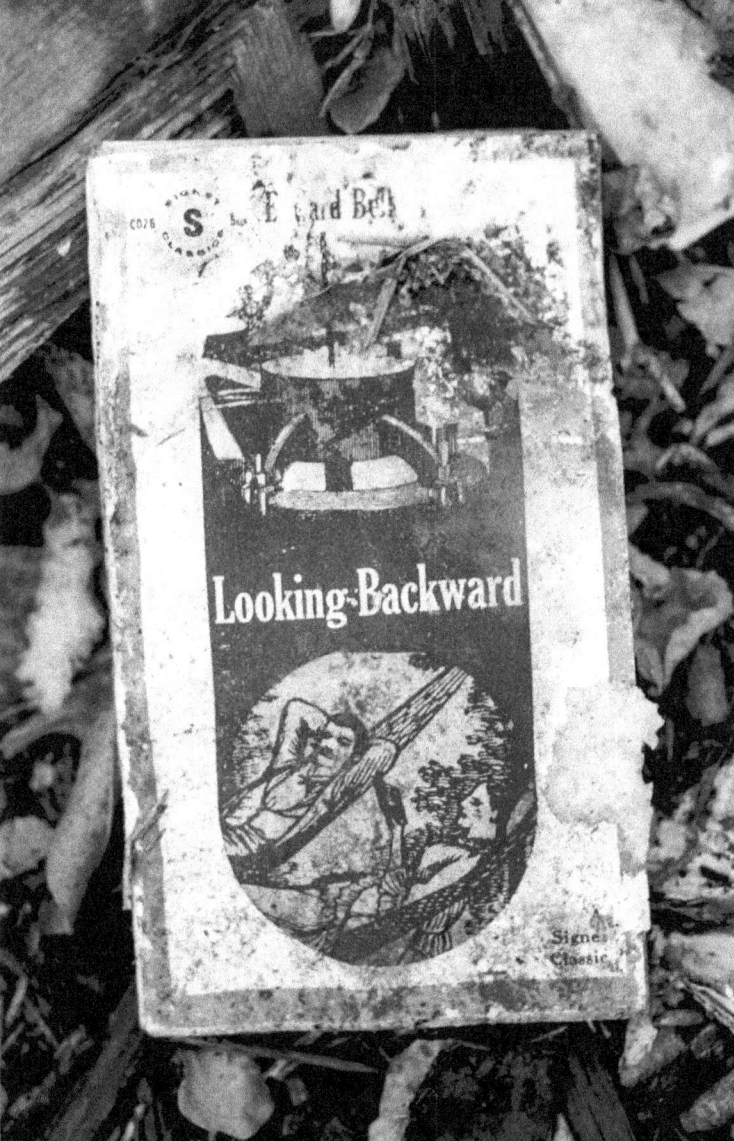

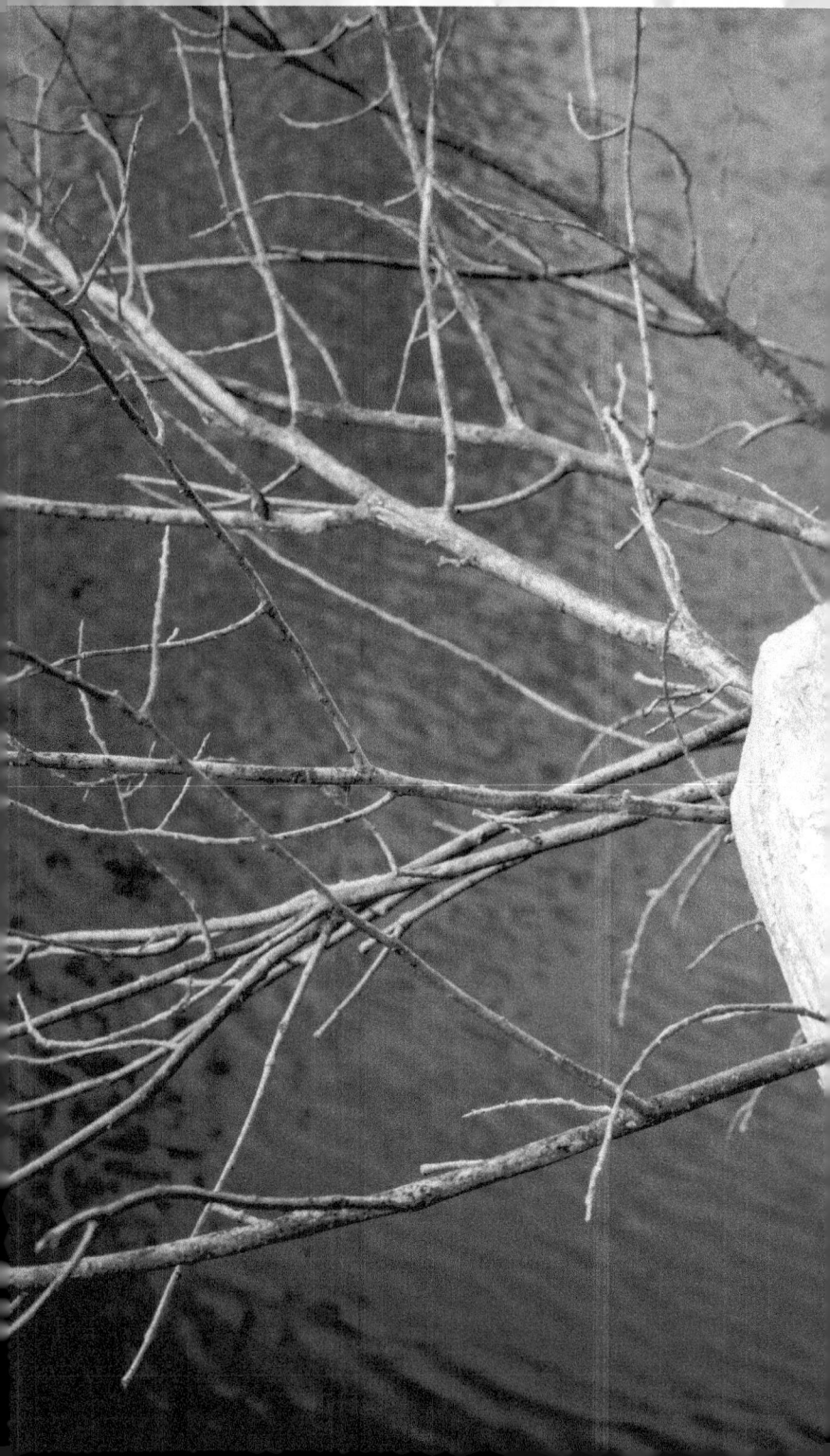

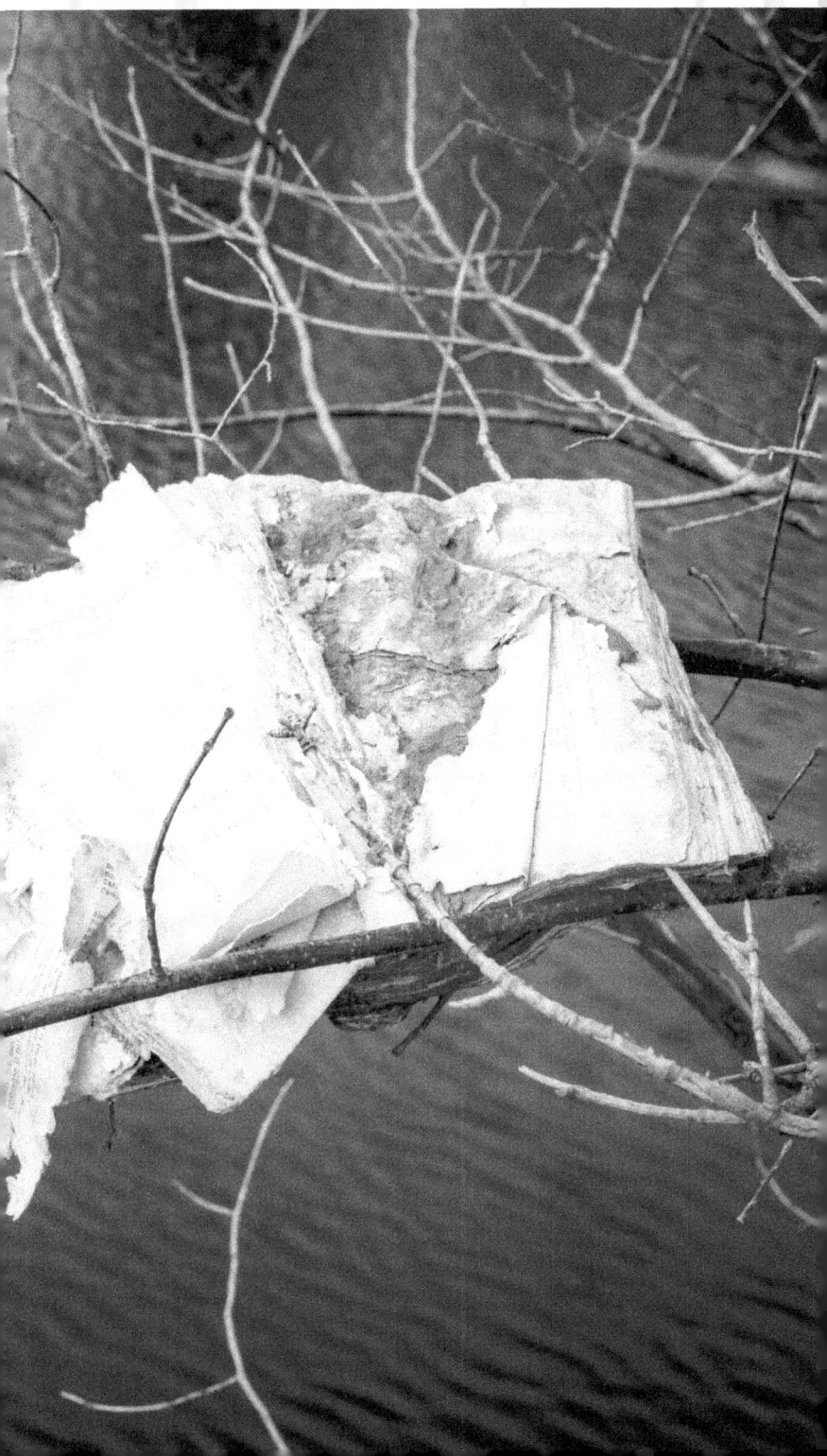

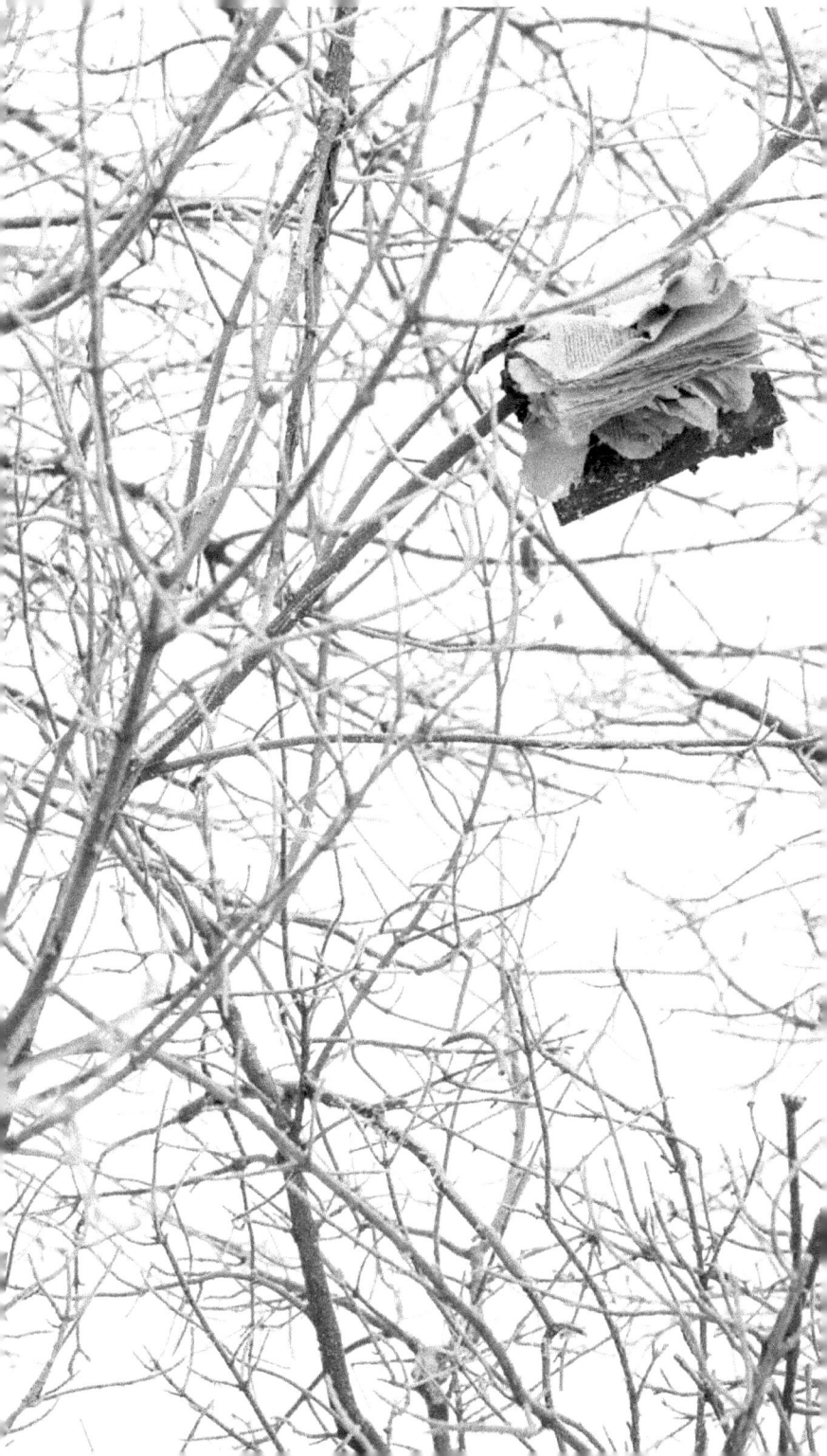

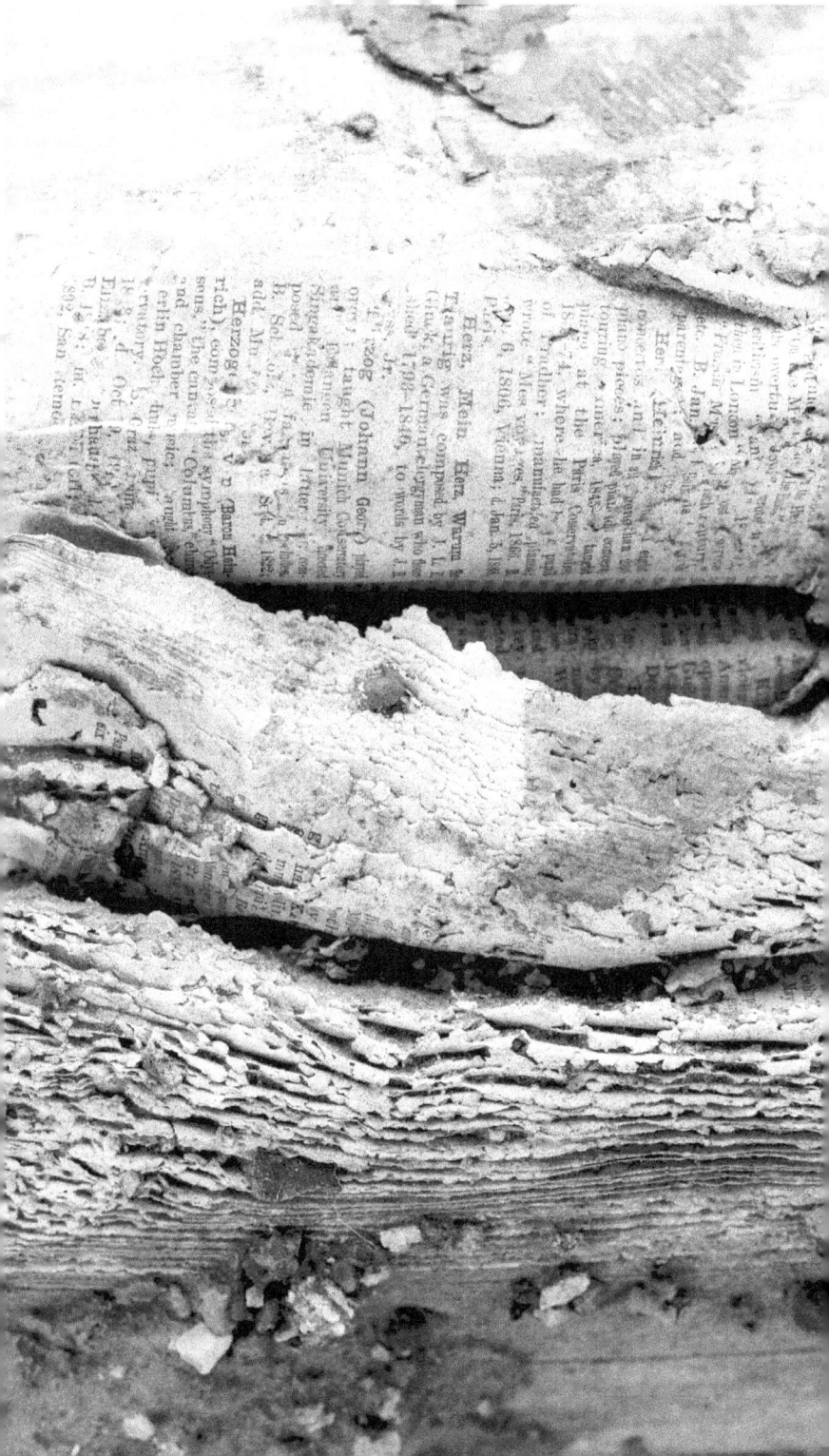

Her. (Heinrich)
piano pieces; his wo... ... et
toujours sincere. D. 18...
phony at the Paris Conserv...
18.. 4, where he had ... rel
of Wagner; manifested ...
wrote a New York ... N. 186..
...y. 6, 1806, Vienna, d. Jan. 5, 18...
Paris...

Herz, Mein Herz, Warm ...
Traurig was composed by J. L. ...
Gluck, a German clergyman who ...
died 1795-1846, to words by ...

...tzog, Jr.
...gen, taught Munich Conserva...
at ... Bonn... Leipsic Universit...
Singakademie in later ...
posed ... Colonists' sing...
... Sel... Trag... Ser... les...
adik. Mu...

Herzog (Johann Georg) pu...
Herzog (... Vn (Barn Heb-
rich), com-pos... for symphony (b)...
sous...; the cantata ... Bir...
...ad chamber ... piece, a violin ...
...erlin Hoch (in), pupil ...
...ervatory. B. G... at ... m...
Edinburgh ... d. Neuhaus ...
R. 148; M. L. I...; C. (off)...
892; San Clemen...

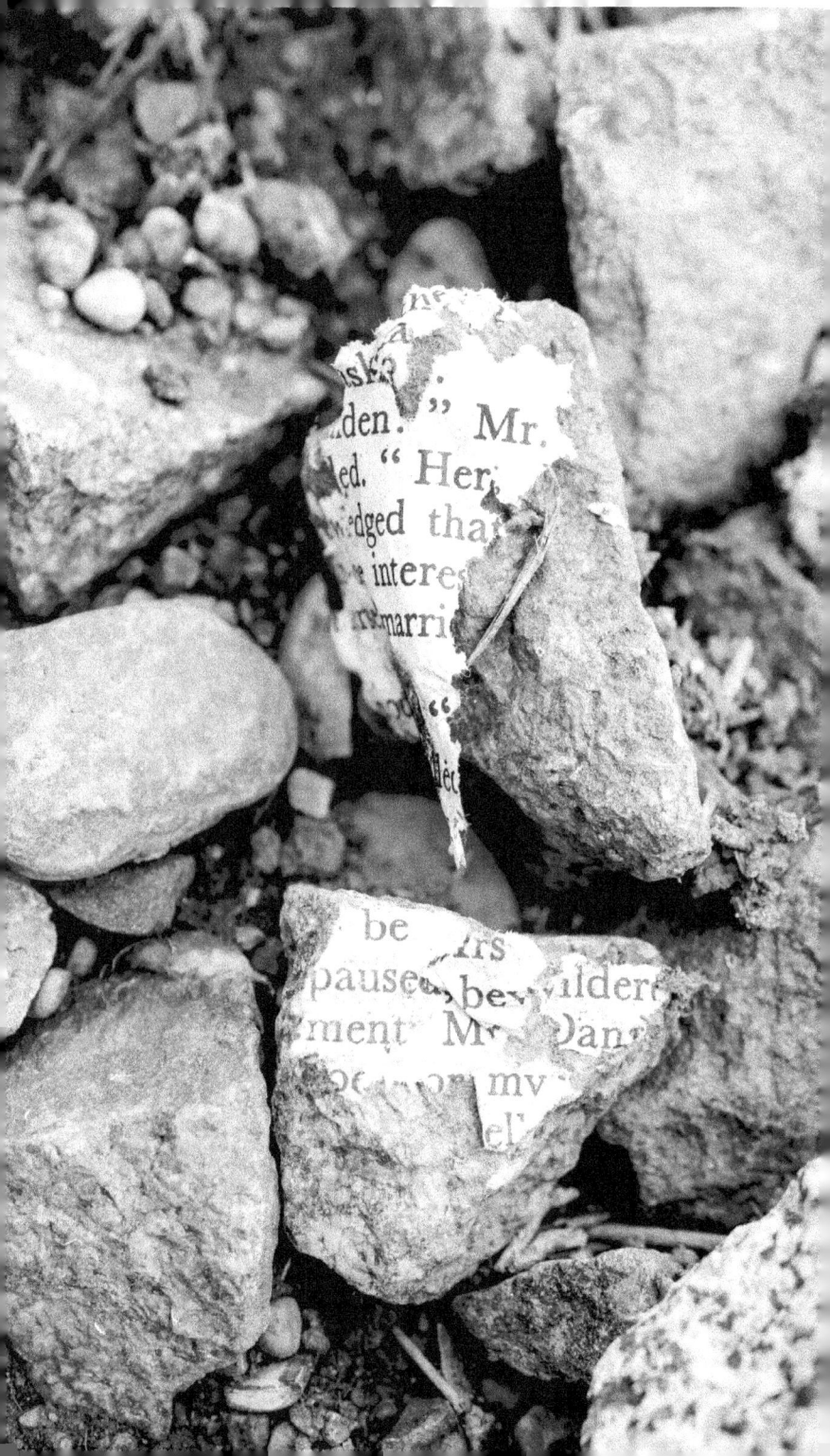

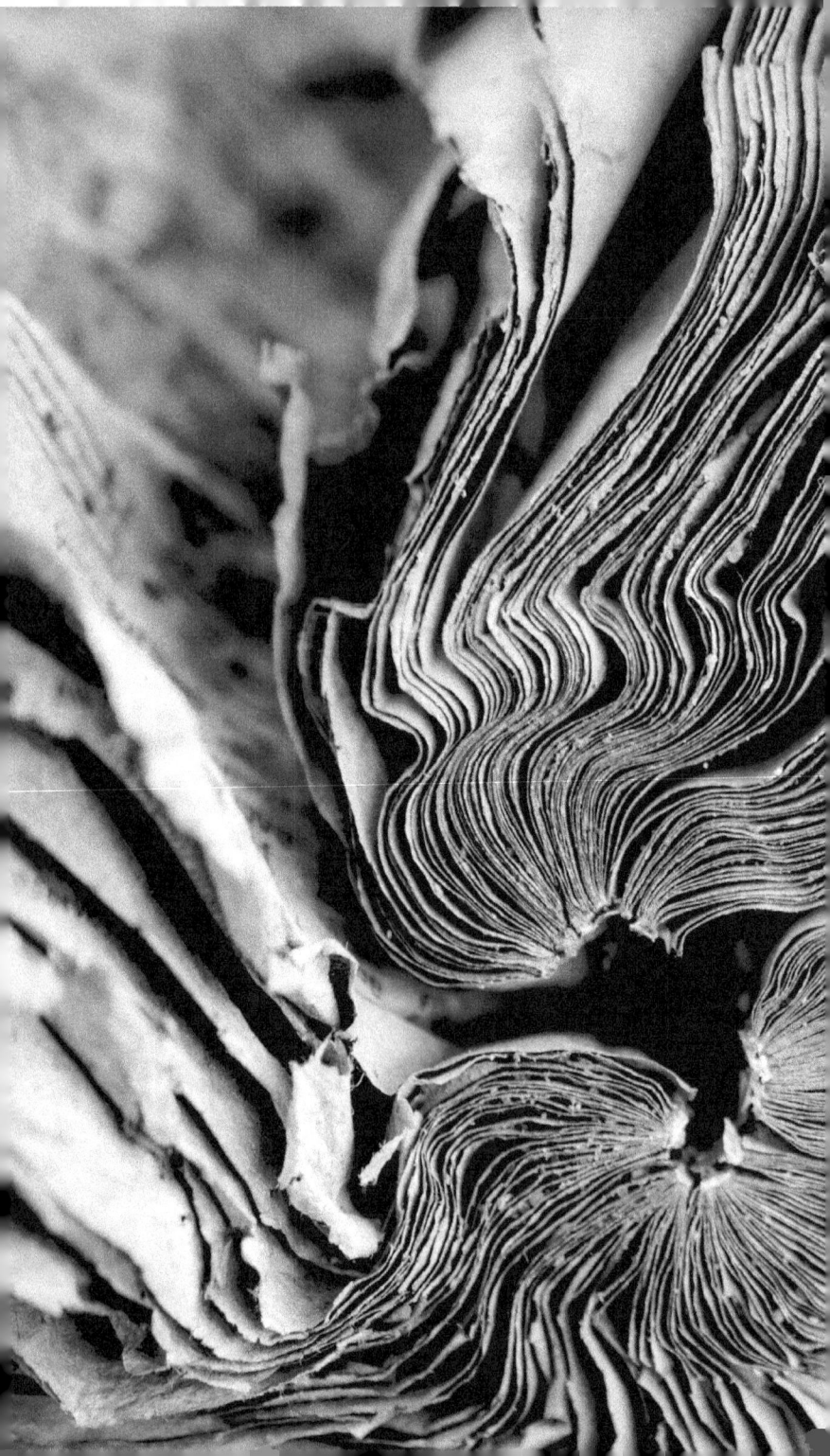

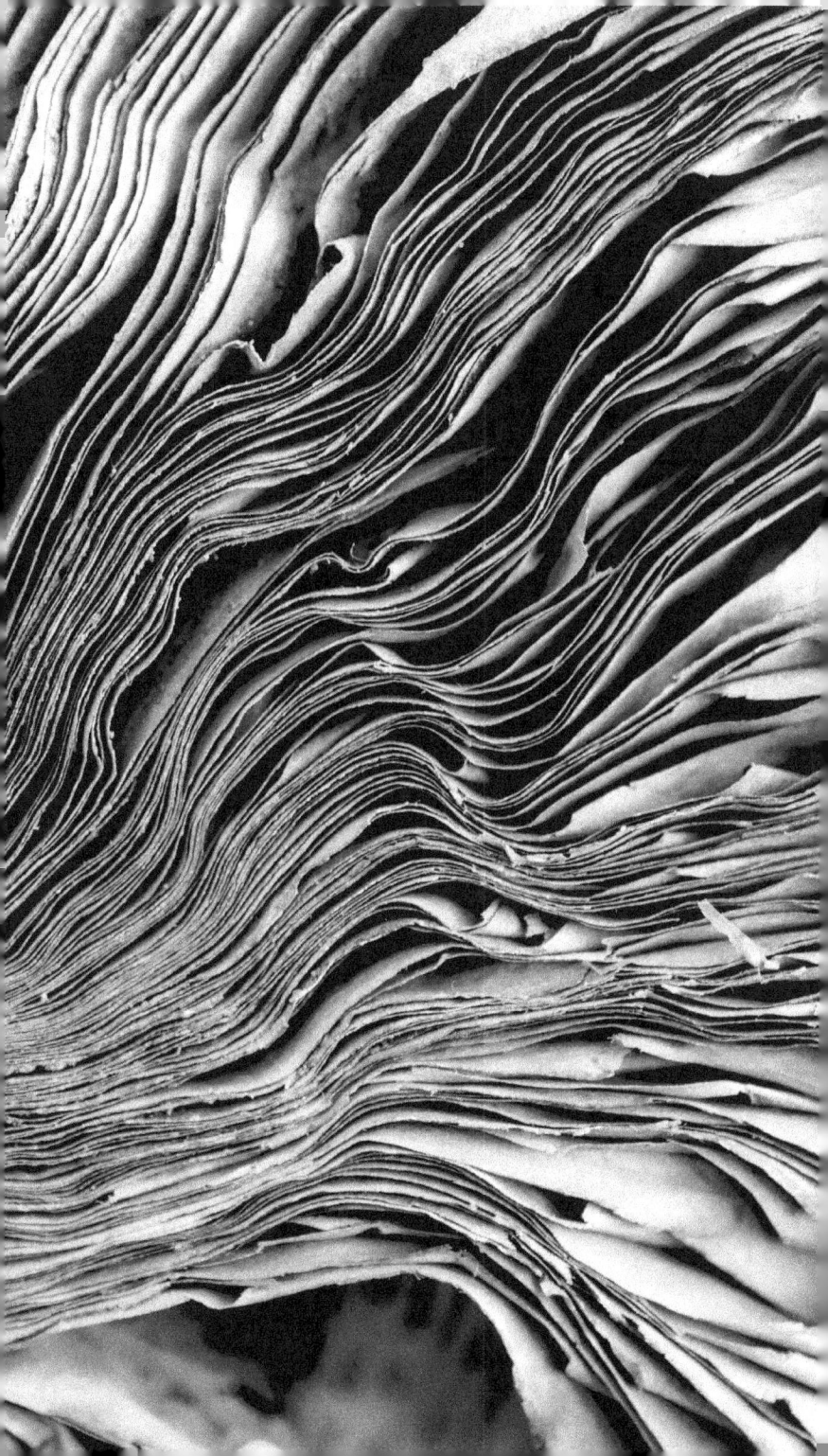

519

MARCO
POLO
IF YOU

'WILL
IF THE
WHOL

'BUCK
NEVER

HERS OF BARD, CAMELOT, FOCUS AND FLARE BOOKS

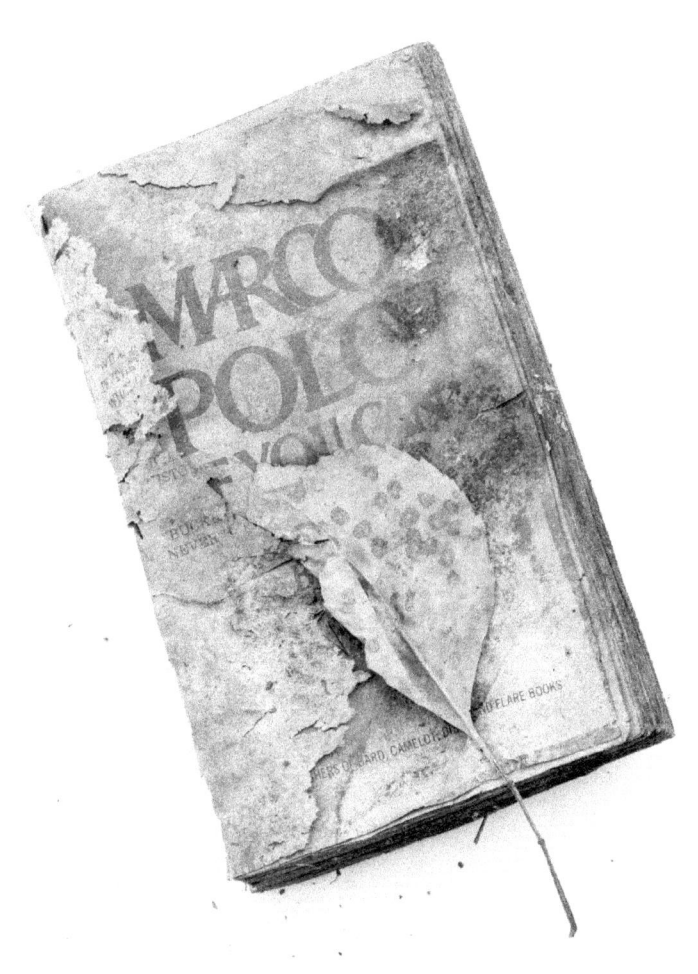

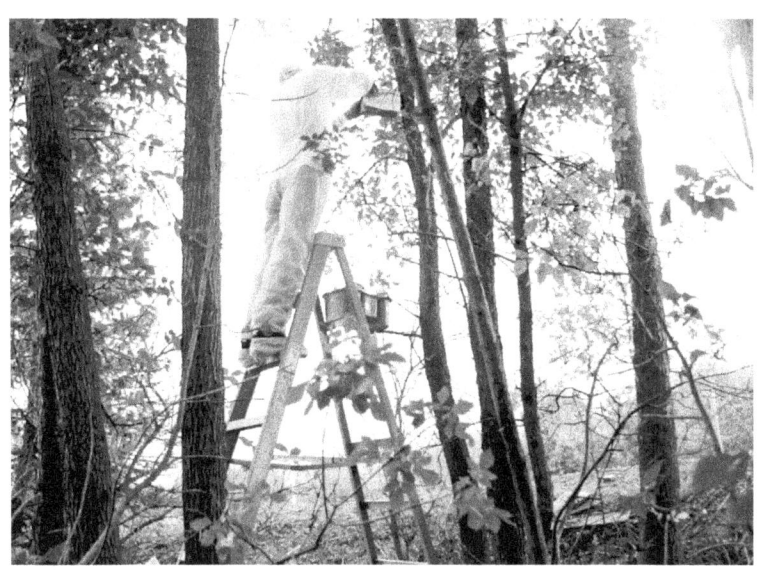

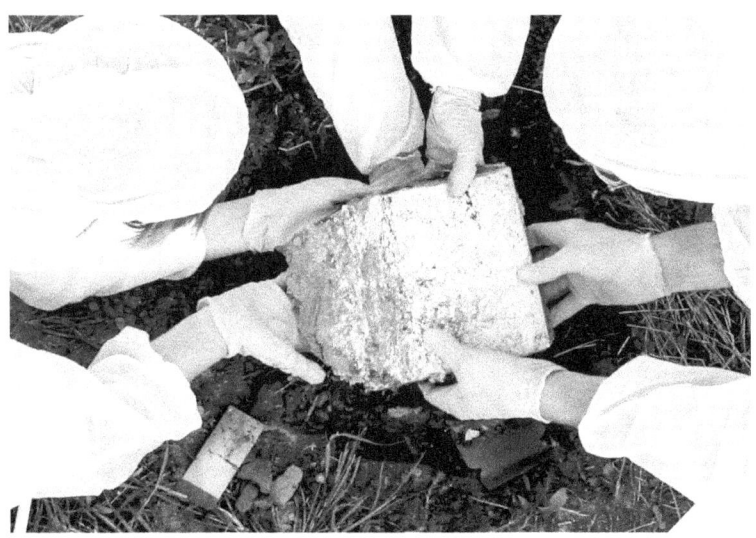

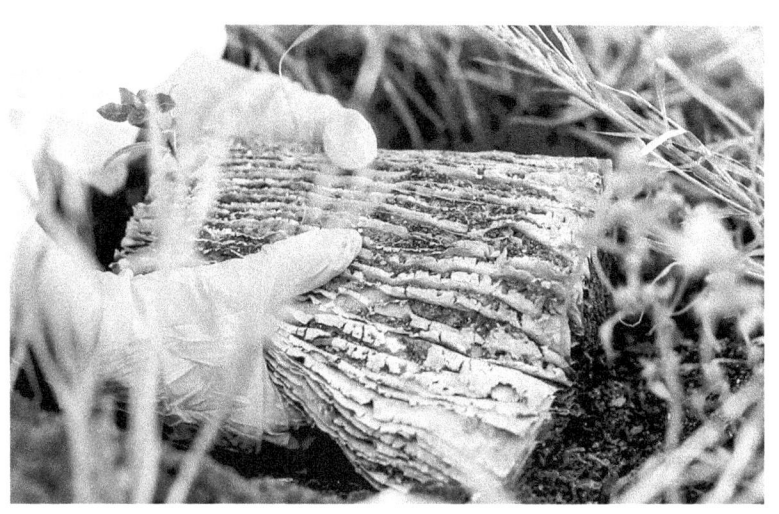

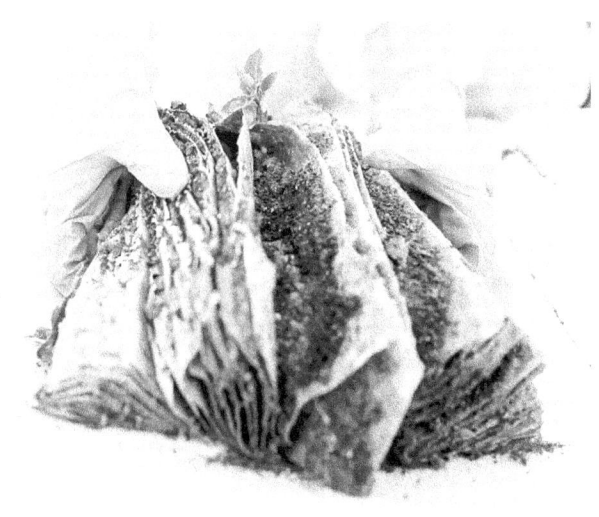

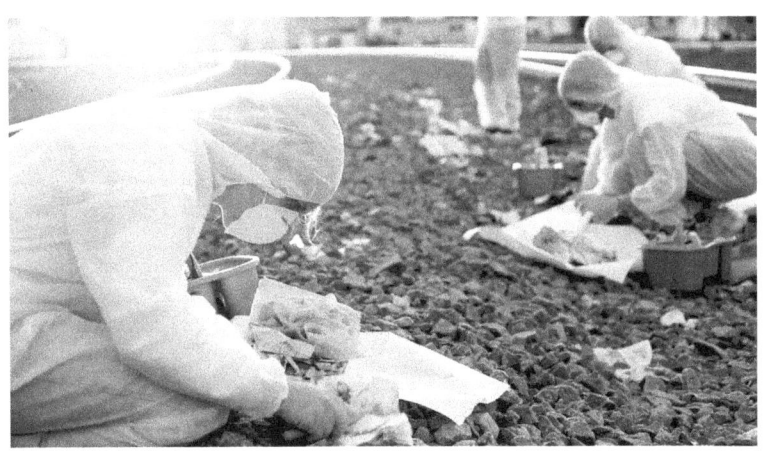

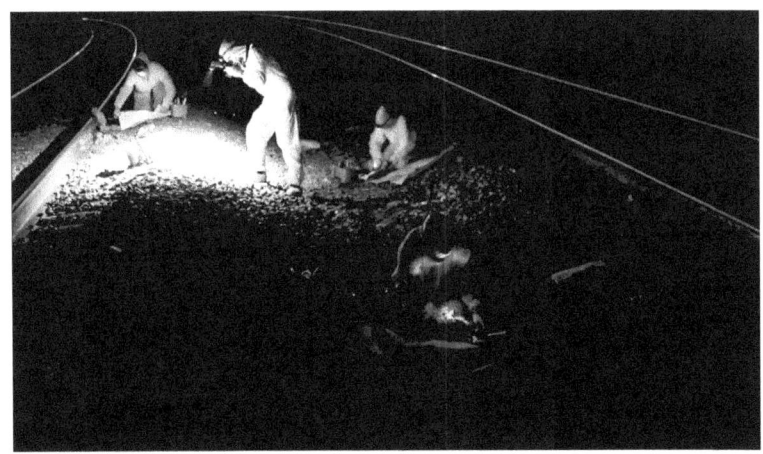

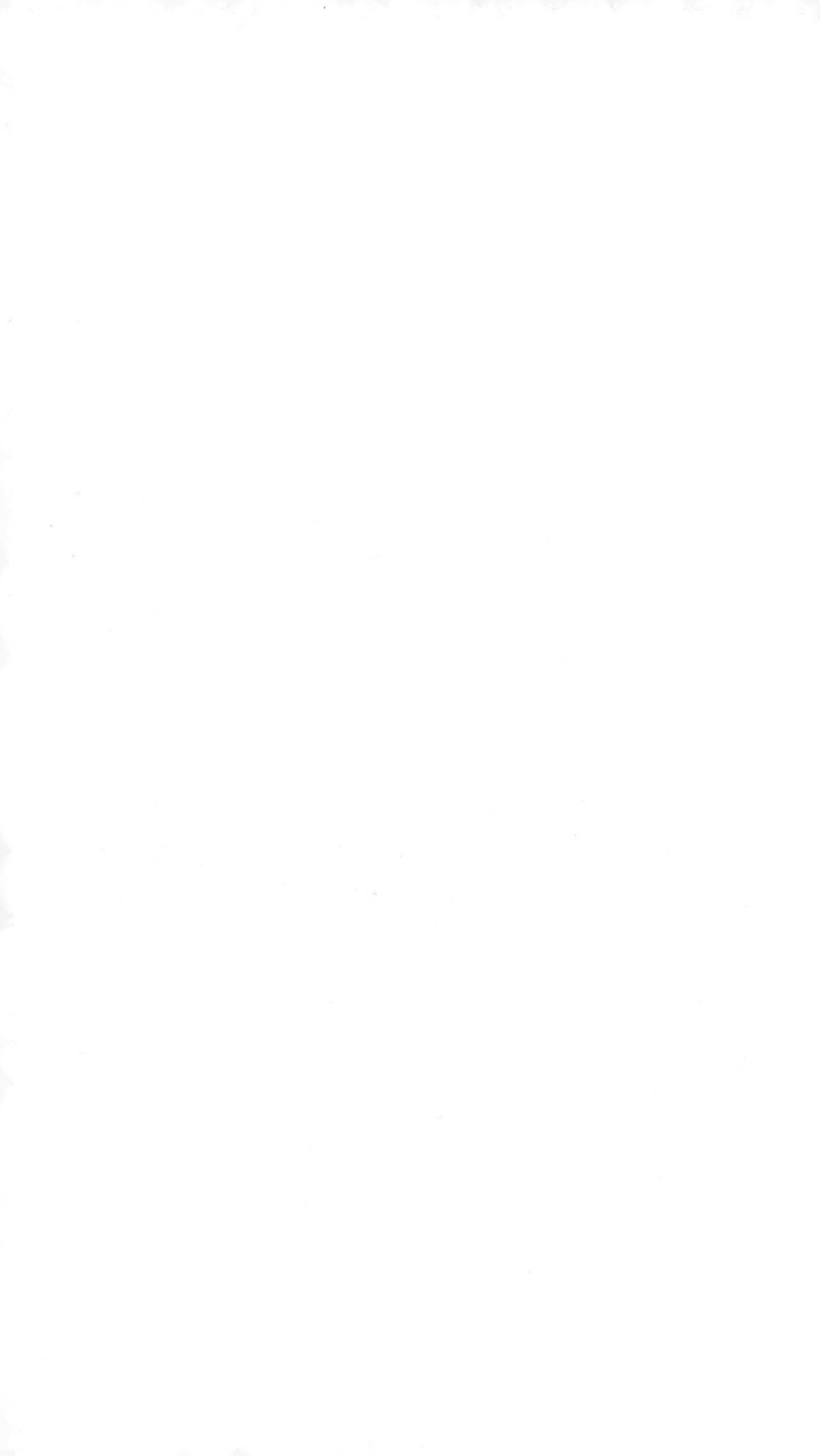

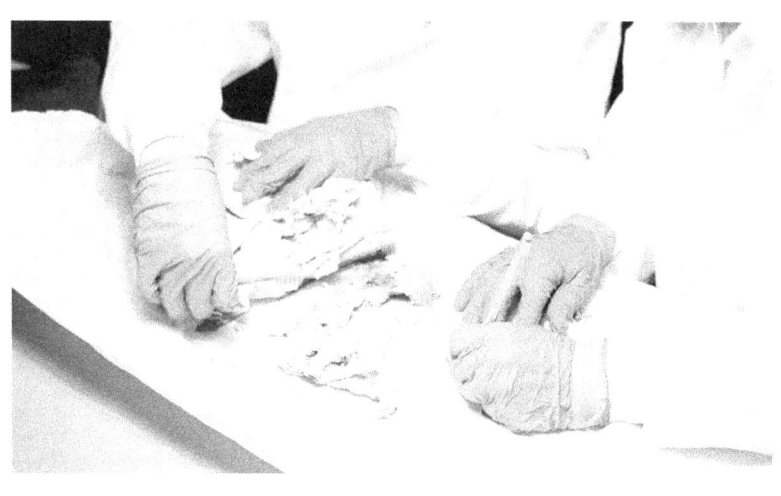

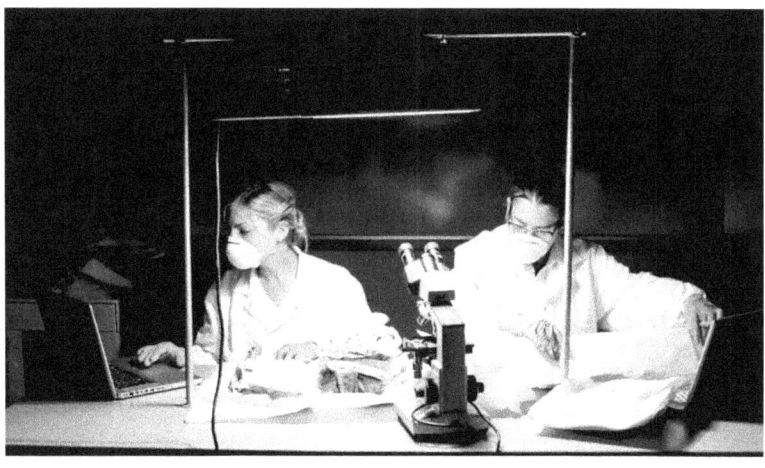

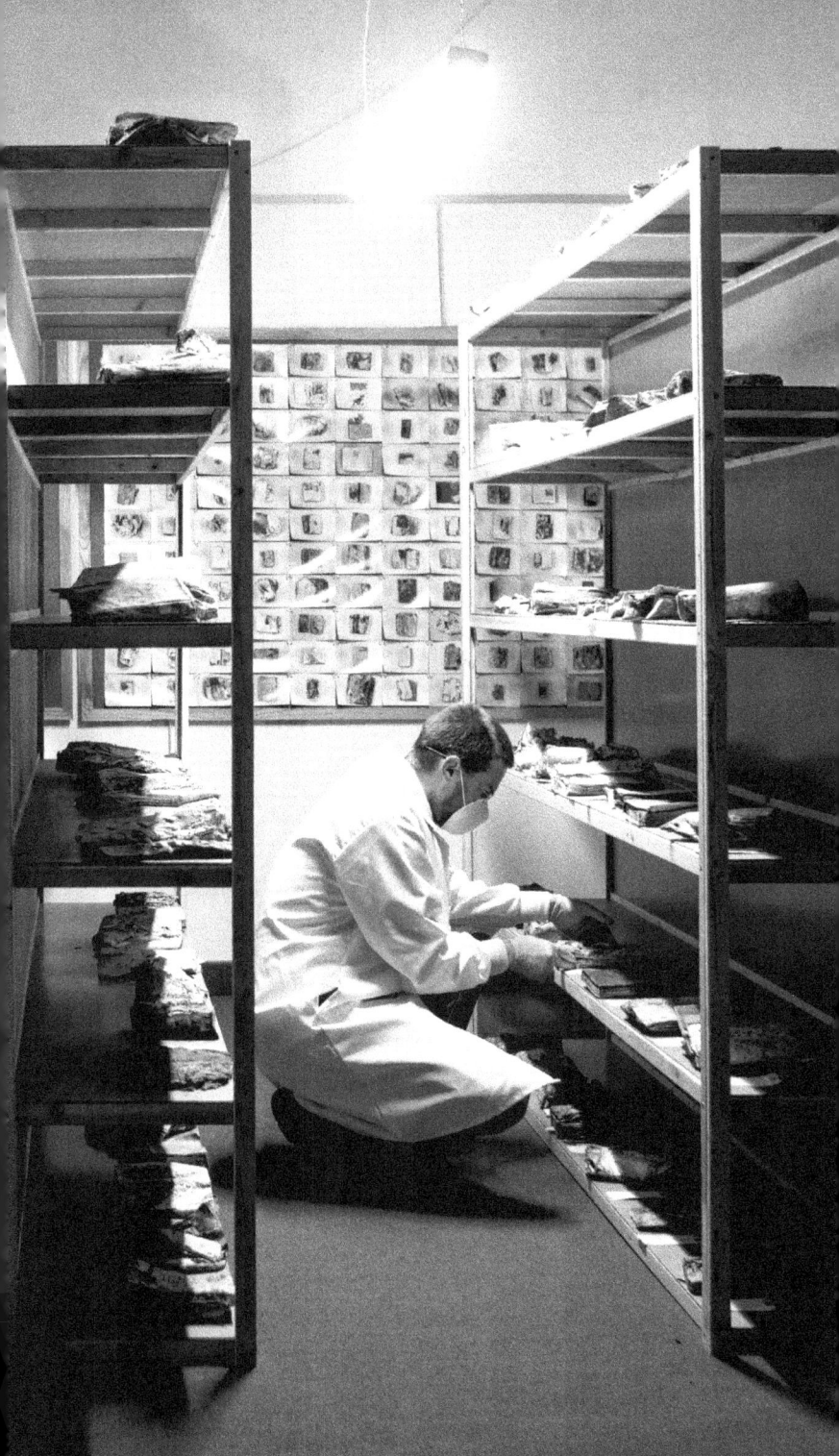

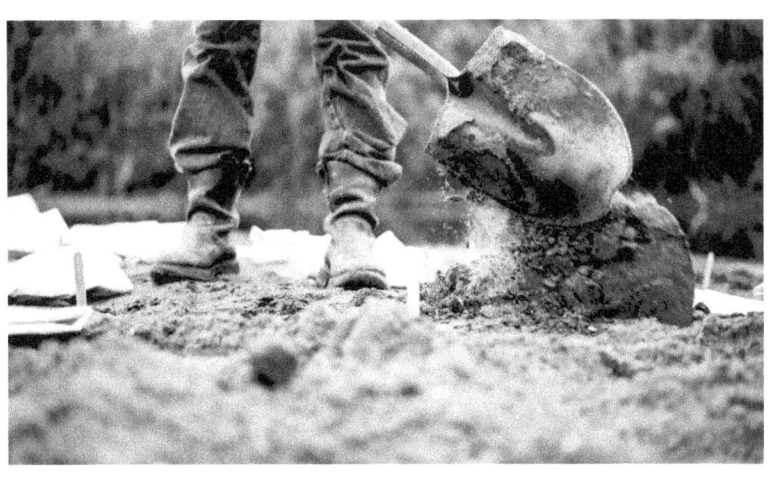

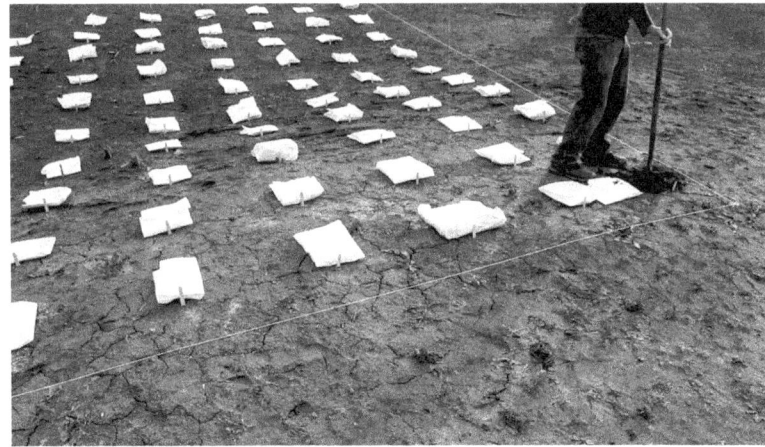

Contributors

Bethany Andreasen

Bethany Andreasen is a Professor of History at Minot State University, where she has taught since 1991. She specializes in American social and cultural history, and is currently engaged in a comparative history project examining the development of normal schools in North Dakota and Saskatchewan from 1890 to 1930. She is also involved with the field of public history, has worked with numerous students on a variety of local history projects, and is the founder and director of the Digital Minot Project, an on-line museum of local history.

Thora Brylowe

Thora Brylowe is an assistant professor of British Romanticism and print history at the University of Colorado, Boulder. Her current book project examines a group of professional printers, authors, editors, painters and engravers, who worked in and around London during the late eighteenth and early nineteenth centuries. She is interested in the labor that goes into making and mediating literature and art, and she has started a new project about the history of papermaking in Britain.

William Caraher

William Caraher is an Associate Professor of History at the University of North Dakota and the publisher of The Digital Press at the University of North Dakota. His research interests include Early Christian and Late Antique Greece and Cyprus, workforce housing in the Bakken oil patch, and public humanities and publishing.

David Haeselin

David Haeselin, PhD, is an instructor in the English department at the University of North Dakota. His scholarship engages the history and future of the book. His recent work appears in Critique: Studies in Contemporary Fiction, Hybrid Pedagogy, and The Los Angeles Review of Books. His edited collection Haunted by Waters: The Future of Memory and the Red River Flood of 1997 was released in May 2017. The book examines the traces left by of the 1997 flood and was co-edited by students in UND's writing, editing, and publishing program.

Robert E. Kibler

Robert E. Kibler, Phd. Native of Takoma Park, Maryland. Studies in Latin Antiquity, Medieval Europe, Classical Chinese Philosophy. Saint Mary's College of Maryland, University of Maryland-College Park, University of Minnesota-Twin Cities. Lived and taught in Beijing, PRC. Teaches at Minot State University. Chair, Foreign Languages, Humanities, Literature. Daughters Cheyenne and Bethany, son Julian, wife Alexandra. Farmer, beekeeper, swimmer, writer.

Sheila Liming

Sheila Liming is Assistant Professor of English at the University of North Dakota, where she teaches classes on American literature and print culture. Her writing has appeared in venues like The Atlantic, The Los Angeles Review of Books, and The Chronicle of Higher Education and her first book, which examines practices of book-collecting and information hoarding in early twentieth-century America, is forthcoming from the University of Iowa Press.

Brian Prugh

Brian Prugh has an MFA in painting from the University of Iowa, where he also studied art history, and an MA in philosophy from the University of Chicago. He exhibits work nationally and writes art criticism regularly for The Seen, an international art journal based in Chicago. He currently lives with his wife and three children in St. Louis and Florida.

Laurel Reuter

Laurel Reuter is the Founding Director of the North Dakota Museum of Art where she also serves as Chief Curator. She was born and raised on the Spirit Lake Dakota Reservation in North Dakota. She received an MA in American literature from the University of North Dakota in 1977, and as a graduate student—again in literature—established the University Art Galleries in the University Student Union that evolved into North Dakota's first art museum, the North Dakota Museum of Art. She has curated dozens of exhibitions by regional, national and international artists and directed numerous artistic commissions.

Justin Sorensen

Justin Sorensen is an artist and writer based in Ohio. Originally from northwestern Pennsylvania, Sorensen received his BFA from Kutztown University in Kutztown, PA, and completed his MFA at the Rhode Island School of Design in Providence, RI. His work has been shown nationally and internationally in the United States, Canada, and Japan.

Ryan Stander

Ryan Stander, is an Assistant Professor of Art at Minot State University where he teaches photography, directs the BFA program, and co-directs Flat Tail Press. Originally from the farmlands of northwest Iowa, Stander is a transplant to central North Dakota. His education alternated between art and theology [MFA from the University of North Dakota, MA in Theology from Sioux Falls Seminary (SD), and a BA in Art from Northwestern College (IA)]. His research interests reside in conversations of art and theology with memory, place, and landscape.

The Digital Press at the University of North Dakota is a collaborative press that works closely with authors and editors to produce innovative academic and popular works. With Micah Bloom's *Codex*, the Digital Press presented an ambitious project that spans media (digital text, video, hardcover, and paperback), embraces archaeological sensibilities, and is both universal and profoundly local in its attention to the flood that devastated Minot in 2011. This trade book version combines Micah Bloom's photography with nine new essays inspired by *Codex*.